What if?

What if?

Mark Manion

aventine press

Published by Aventine Press
55 East Emerson St.
Chula Vista CA 91911
www.aventinepress.com

ISBN: 978-1-59330-986-2

Printed in the United States of America

Table of Contents

What If...

Have you ever thought, 'Wow! I must be dreaming. When am I going to wake up?' Maybe you are living a fairy-tale life, one you never imagined possible, at least not for you. Everything seems to be going right. You've got a to-die-for mate, a great job, a beautiful home, and a stock portfolio that's gone through the roof. You're healthy. You have a gym membership and even time to work out three days a week. Your children love you, and the dog does too! And, as if that's not enough, you just won the lottery! Pinch me. Can this be real?

Or maybe you are living a horrific life. Terrible things just keep happening to you, and seemingly for no good reason at all. Each day is a dreadful experience. Your spouse is both verbally and physically abusive to you, you're about to get laid off from your job, the bank's foreclosing on your house, and the stocks you own aren't worth the cost of the paper they're printed on. You accidentally backed into a gym with your car causing major damage, only to find out that your auto insurance had expired two months ago. Your kids are juvenile delinquents, the cat too. It just scratched a hole through your soft leather sofa. Please wake me up from this nightmare!

Or maybe your life fits somewhere in between this heaven and hell spectrum.

Well, what if?

What if one day you woke up to find that the last five, ten, twenty, however many years of your life, had all been a dream? What if you woke up to find that you aren't really old, that you haven't lost your teeth, you're not laboring to walk because of creaky joints, and you haven't attended your spouses' funeral? What if you woke up to find you've been dreaming? That you couldn't have lost a spouse because you've never been married. In fact, what if you woke up to find that you are still in junior high school, and the thought of even dating someone makes you break out in a cold sweat?

Well, what if... ?

Chapter One

Pizza Plunge

I t was January 13, 1991. I looked down at my watch. 'Oh my goodness, I'm running late.' I called home.

"Hello," my bride answered.

"Honey, I'll be home in a jif. A couple more minutes here and I'm out the door."

"Jane arrived over an hour ago. We're waiting. And we're hungry!" Priscilla responded, somewhat perturbed at my tardiness.

"Sorry I'm late. Call Little Caesars© and order two pizzas. I'll pick them up on my way home."

"We'll go get them," she offered.

"No, I'll get them," I insisted. "It's on my way. Why waste the gas?"

"Okay, I'll see you when you get here. I love you."

"Ditto."

Priscilla and I owned a residential care home for developmentally disabled adults. I was the administrator and had been giving some instructions to our manager. This business, along with being back in school working on a degree in psychology, kept me extremely busy. Not to mention that we already had two baby girls under 18 months old and we'd only been married a couple of years. It was hectic! Robyn and Rochelle were our two bundles of joy, definitely worth all the hard work. Priscilla's friend, Jane, had come down from San Bernardino to help with them.

I said good-bye to our manager and headed out the door. 'Wow, it's awfully dark right here,' I thought as I struggled to walk to my car. 'The porchlight must've burned out.'

I walked with a cane because of muscle weakness and balance problems. Nighttime was particularly challenging because I depended on my vision for balance. Walking in the dark was almost impossible for me. All this, and much much more, the result of a broken neck I suffered many years earlier, s-i-x-t-e-e-n of them to be exact, but who's counting. My best friend, my cousin Mike, and I had been on a cross-country bicycle trip. It was only the fourth day of our journey when it happened. A drunk driver plowed into both of us, killing Mike and leaving my life forever changed. That fateful day was August 7, 1974.

I made it to my car and drove to the pizza outlet. When I arrived I was somewhat relieved; the parking lot was well lit. As I walked towards the entrance another challenging thought hit me, 'How am I going to carry two large pizzas back to my car? My left arm barely works and I have to hold my cane with my right hand. I guess I can ask for help.' How unlike me was that, I mean, to ask for help? I had been a fiercely independent individual. Some might have even said hard-headed, but age was starting to soften me.

I pushed open the glass door and began to walk in. Instantly, something grabbed my left foot just as I let go of the door. I quickly glanced down. 'Oh crap!' My foot was trapped beneath the doormat. Stumbling forward, I desperately tried to regain my balance. My cane went flying. One step, two, and then *BAM!!* I had torpedoed head first into the counter where I was supposed to pick up my pizzas. My head snapped back. *CRACK!* It hit the floor and split open. 'Manion, you idiot, how could you let something like this happen to you,' I scolded myself.

The manager dashed to my aid and told me not to move. I couldn't feel anything from my neck down so that wasn't going to be a problem. I didn't have a clue where my arms or legs were. After calling 911 he asked, "Is there anybody else you'd like me to call?"

"Yes, you better call my wife. She's going to wonder why I'm late. She isn't gonna like this."

My head bleeding, lying there on the cold tiled floor, I waited for the ambulance to arrive. I knew I'd broken my neck again. Deja vu! It was hard to believe that this could be happening to me again. I mean, breaking your neck once is huge, but twice? And in the same lifetime? This was crazy. This couldn't be happening. The florescent lights overhead began to flicker. I felt a little tired, a little groggy. 'I'll simply close my eyes,' I thought, 'and when I open them, all of this will just have been a bad dream.'

Chapter Two

Day Four Do Over

Feeling uncomfortably warm I opened my eyes. I looked up and something very, very strange had occurred. There were no florescent lights flickering above. There was no counter next to me, and no manager peering down at me, only open space. Still groggy, I wondered, 'Where am I?' I was completely disoriented. The light that was striking me was from the sun peaking over the distant mountains. I was a little rattled. No, I was in shock! Then it dawned on me, I'd been dreaming! The fall at Little Caesars©, the bike crash — they never happened. Immediately I sat up. I wasn't paralyzed. I really had been dreaming. I lifted my arms over my head. I couldn't believe it!! They worked, and I could even wiggle all my fingers. A joy burst inside me. Unable to contain myself I jumped to my feet, and I jumped and I jumped and I jumped some more. I could actually jump without falling. This was so incredible, so amazingly bizarre. I looked over and there was my best friend, my cousin Mike, still asleep in his sleeping bag. He was breathing. He wasn't dead. I was so happy. I was fully awake now. Mike really wasn't dead and I really wasn't paralyzed. The feeling was euphoric. A great sense of relief came over me.

"Hey Mike, let's get a move on it," I hollered. There was no response. 'Should I?' I thought. 'Yeah, why not?' I answered myself. "Blah!!" I yelled as I jumped on his sleeping bag. It shook him up real good.

"Hey! You could've given me a heart attack," my momentarily frightened buddy gasped.

"Oh yeah, just be thankful it was only me. I could have been a mugger. If we don't get moving soon, we'll die frying in the sun. A heart attack would be an easy way out."

"Just remember, Grandpa and Grandma had them, and so did your dad."

"Get over it. You've got a lot of livin' ahead of you, except for…"

"Except for what?"

"My dream."

"Your dream?"

"Yeah. Mike, I had the most horrific dream last night. It was so vivid. I felt it. I'm telling you, it seemed real."

"So what about your dream?" Mike wanted to know. "Hey, wait a minute. Is this another one of your jokes?"

"No, I'm serious Mike. You've heard about dreams coming true sometimes, haven't you? You know, like a premonition."

"I have," he answered warily.

"Well, in my dream, you died."

"I died?"

"Yeah, you died. We were hit by a drunk driver. You were killed and I was left totally paralyzed. I recovered somewhat only to break my neck again years later. I tripped on a mat when walking into a pizza joint. And get this, I was married and had two kids."

"You are whacko."

"Whacko or not, it seemed so real, almost prophetic or something. The images, the emotions, they've set up camp in my head. It's like a major motion picture in my brain. I still feel it, like it really happened. And I'm sorry about jumpin' on you. That's no way to treat my dyin' buddy. I won't do that again. I don't know what came over me."

"You're right, you will be sorry. I owe you one, dreamer. What's up with me getting killed and you surviving?"

"Dude, it was my dream. Wait'll I tell you about it. You may be glad you didn't have to go through some of the stuff I did. There were times when I thought you were the lucky one."

"Sounds interesting. We'll talk as we ride," Mike said. "You like writing. Maybe you should write a book or try making a movie."

"Maybe."

Mike rode his bike into town to get some sweet rolls and milk. When he returned we ate, packed, cleaned the area where we'd camped, and then thanked the police officers who'd been so kind to us. They'd told the groundskeeper not to water the area where we stayed. We were grateful. Sprinklers popping up and dousing us in the middle of the night would have been a real pain in the butt. Our pedaling began. We felt rested and wonderful, but could tell it was going to be a scorching hot day.

This was the fourth day of our cross-country bicycle trip, one that we'd been planning for seven months. It was to take us from San Diego, through California, all the way to Chico in the northern part of our state. Mike's brother, Chuck, lived there. Once there, we planned on doing some backpacking at Mount Shasta with him and some inner-tubing down the Sacramento River. Then we'd continue riding east over to Boise, Idaho, where a girl friend of mine lived. She was going to show us around that area. After that, our route had us riding all the way to Ely, Minnesota, way up by the Canadian border. It's where our grandparents lived. We'd made arrangements to purchase a canoe once we got there. Canoe-camping up into Canada for a few weeks was going to be the perfect climax to our 2,400 mile journey. We were on one of those killer, once-in-a-lifetime adventures! One, that God willing, we'd love to recount to our future kids and grandkids.

Mike and I had worked hard to put this trip together. The timing was right for a journey of this extent because neither one of us was tied down yet to career, family, or school. The only stickler was our girlfriends. They weren't too crazy about the idea of us leaving them for three and a half months. Come to think of it, neither were our moms. I clearly remember one particular evening at my mom's house before we left on our trip. Up drove my cousins, Janine, Mike, and their younger sister, Lynette. My Aunt Jean, or AJ as I more affectionately like to call her, was with them. They happened to be in the area and popped in to say hello.

We all sat around the kitchen table and chatted about Mike's and my upcoming trip. We talked about Mike's harrowing weeks with bicycle dealers, trying to get some needed parts. And we talked about the farewell party we were throwing together for family and close friends. Finally, our conversation changed to movies and the new hit called 'Deliverance' starring Burt Reynolds. It was a horrifying, action-packed thriller about a nice, little canoe-camping trip gone bad. It had rogue thugs, people getting killed, overturned canoes in violent rapids, and mangled bodies, one guy with his leg hanging on by a piece of skin. This movie definitely had you on the edge of your seat. I'd just seen it and so had Mike.

"Well, Mike," I'd asked jokingly, "do you still want to do the canoeing part of our trip? You know we're bound to run into some rapids, and who knows, maybe even a couple of mentally deranged back-woodsmen."

Mike laughed. "Get outta here. That kinda stuff only happens in movies."

"Yeah, but we really will have to deal with some rapids," I continued, trying to egg him on.

"That we most certainly will," Mike replied undaunted. "They'll be a blast."

"But what if our canoe capsizes?" I asked, still trying to stir something up.

My aunt pounced on that one. "Yeah, what *if* you're canoe capsizes?" She was getting worried. Mom had even started to look concerned.

"We're not going to capsize," Mike responded. I nodded my head in agreement.

"But what are you going to do if you do?" AJ insisted. "I think you ought to skip the canoe-camping and just stay around your grandparents' lake."

"We're not going to capsize," I reaffirmed. "I'm just teasing you. We've got good heads on our shoulders and we intend to keep them there. We'll do things safely!"

"But what if you do?" my mom repeated.

'Well, it looks like I really got a hornets' nest stirred up now,' I thought. 'This probably isn't too wise of me. Our conversation has gotten out of hand.' "We are NOT going to capsize," I said again, "but if we do, it will all depend on several factors."

"What factors?" AJ and Mom asked in unison.

I looked over at my cousin Janine for some kind of help. She just looked at me like, hey, you got yourself into this mess, good luck getting out of it. "Okay, okay, it would depend on if one of us got hurt, and if so, how badly," I started babbling, purposely blowing everything out of proportion. "Let's just say we overturned in some rapids and I struck a rock and my leg was almost cut off and I was bleeding to death and was in intense pain, and it looked like I was going to die without help soon or lose my leg. Or if I got paralyzed and couldn't walk and we were too far from civilization — mind you, this isn't going to happen, but if it did — I would want to die. I would want Mike to finish me off, you know, kill me. If he left to get help I'd probably die anyway and I wouldn't want to become a meal for a bear or any other wild animal." I looked at Mike and said, "If I get as bad as that, I want you to kill me, okay? There is no way I want to live the rest of my life paralyzed, in a wheelchair, with people always having to help me. I'd be better off dead, and with a little luck, up in heaven."

"I agree," Mike responded. "I'd never want to live my life in a wheelchair either. If I get wrecked up that bad or worse and we are a couple of days from help and things are looking helpless, I want you to kill me too."

"Agreed," I replied. With that all said and done, Mike and I shook hands on it. My mom and my aunt sat there wide-eyed and ashen looking. I'm sure they could not have believed what they were hearing. Any fears they'd had were definitely amplified. Bleeding to death, paralyzed, helpless, intense pain, killing one another — these words did not exactly make a fearful parent feel at ease.

I quickly jumped back into the conversation, "Hey, hey, this is getting absurd. These kinds of things only happen in movies. Whatever it is you're imagining, believe me, it ain't gonna happen. Mike and I are intelligent guys. We'll use caution. There's absolutely nothing for you to worry about. After all, Mike's 18 and out of high school, and I'm 19 and have already finished my first year of college. We're not little kids anymore."

We had our folks pretty shook up that night, our moms at least. Mike's dad was out of the loop since his parents' separation, and my dad had died two years earlier of a heart attack. The first night of our trip we'd camped in a park overlooking the ocean in Laguna Beach. That was until about 2:00am when a couple of police officers kicked us out.

We missed the 'NO CAMPING' sign. Our second night was spent next to a fire-ring on the beach in Malibu. And last night we camped here in a park by a police station on the outskirts of a little town called Maricopa. How safe was that! So, as you can see, three days on the road and no real incidents, no problems. What were our moms worrying about?

We rode through Maricopa and then headed out into the country. The countryside left a little to be desired from a scenery standpoint. Sagebrush sparsely grew in this mostly barren, oil-stained land. Oil pumps were scattered about. Many of these steel monuments of mankind sat silenced, like massive sledgehammers frozen in time. Others kept ceaselessly cranking, drawing up oil from underground. They made an eerie noise. Pedaling our bikes through this area had become almost a mechanical thing, like the oil pumps, a constant cranking of our pedals and seemingly getting nowhere due to the non-changing landscape. I imagined myself in a 'War of the Worlds' movie where alien beings had caused all this desolation.

The only thing that seemed to keep us in touch with the real world was the occasional complaint Mike and I exchanged about the heat. The temperature had soared to a blazing 100 degrees. The sun's rays glistened off our shirtless bodies, wet with perspiration. Occasionally a drop of sweat would find its way into one of my eyes causing it to sting. The day had gone from a feeling-wonderful morning to a less-than-pleasurable noontime ride.

We rode into a small town. A very, very, small town consisting of a few homes, a combination market/gas station, and a coffee shop. For the life of me I couldn't see why anybody would want to live here or how they could possibly earn enough money to survive. The people were nice though. In fact, I remembered stopping here on another bicycle trip a year earlier. It had been a warm day too. But it had been drizzling and some of our stuff was getting wet. An elderly lady saw our plight, went to her house, and returned with plastic bags to keep our things dry. She also insisted on giving us as much fruit as we could carry. She had a heart of gold. Mike and I didn't run into her this time though. We bought a couple of sodas and some apples, filled our water bottles, and continued on our way.

It kept getting hotter and hotter. About 1:30pm we came upon a public swimming pool. The thermometer there read 103 degrees, in the shade. That's searing, fry your eggs on the sidewalk, hot. There was no question as to what to do. We paid our 50 cent entry fee, asked the girls at the desk to watch our bikes, and went swimming. The first half hour in the pool Mike and I didn't swim. We simply sat there and enjoyed the cool refreshing water.

"Mike, this is so like in my dream. It's spooky," I commented, "Maybe I just remember this place from my past trip with Brett. It can't be though, 'cause we never went swimming on that one. Weird, huh?"

"I don't know, I wasn't there," Mike answered.

"And the girls at the desk, just like in my dream."

"Now you're fantasizing."

"Mike, I'm serious. In my dream we met a couple of girls here. They invited us to a party that night, but we said no and continued on our way. As we rode it got dark. Later on, some lights approached us from behind, and all of a sudden, CRUNCH!! My back tire blew out and my bicycle started buckling right beneath me. I went into slow motion, everything being firmly etched in my mind, the horror of horrors. Both of my ankles snapped. Then the fender of the car ripped into the back of my right thigh, tearing it open right down to the bone. As I was whipped back across the hood of the car, my neck was broken, the force actually causing my skull to get wrenched off my spine. Then I crashed into the windshield, gashing open the back of my left shoulder when it shattered. And finally, some two hundred thirty feet further down the road, what seemed like the length of a football field, THUMP! I landed on the side of the road. It was a hard hit!" I paused for a second, then pondered out-loud, "Hmm, two hundred thirty feet. Why would I have such an accurate number? I'll tell you Mike, it was like I was there."

"Dude, that's one wild dream," Mike responded. "What was it about me getting killed?"

"Well, in the dream, there was an instant more of clanging, twisting metal and then there was silence. A very loud frightening silence. It was so loud I could feel it. My skin was crawling, probably from all the blood. I yelled out for you and there was no answer. I yelled again, and still there was no answer. Dude, I'm sorry, you went under the car and died."

"What do you mean, you're sorry?"

"I'm so sorry. Wait a sec. I think I'm getting an idea for a new song. …I'm so sorry, Uncle … uh, … Uncle … "

"Albert, Albert you idiot. It's already been done."

I smiled.

"But you knew that, didn't you?"

"Yeah. I think it was The Beach Boys."

"Wrong." Mike shook his head.

"I meant The Bee Gees."

"The Beatles. It was The Beatles."

I smiled again.

"But you knew that too, huh? And to think this is only the fourth day of our trip. Yikes!" Mike took a deep breath. "Okay, now why are you so sorry?"

"I didn't get to attend your funeral. I was really messed up. I was in the hospital in critical condition. Wait'll I tell you about that. Again, I'm so sorry."

"Get over it you idiot. It didn't really happen."

"Yeah, you're right. What am I thinking?" I replied, feeling somewhat relieved. Yet it all seemed so real. It got me emotionally worked up.

Mike and I swam around for half an hour, got out, and then ate a big lunch. Refreshed and refueled, we decided that this place was so nice and the day too hot to be riding. We opted to stay put for the rest of the afternoon. Shelly and Lisa, the two friendly and attractive girls who worked there, probably helped in our decision. We watched them play chess for awhile and then all four of us went swimming again. The girls showed us some of the dives they perform in competition. They were looking very good. The dives, I mean. Finally, it was getting towards closing time, so we got out, showered, and put on some fresh clothes. The day was still warm, but at least it was now tolerable.

"I'd like you two to come to a party we're having tonight," Shelly, one of our two new friends offered. "It's at my house over in Bakersfield."

"Yes, why don't you guys come?" Lisa, the other, smiled invitingly.

Mike and I looked at each other. This was too weird. Had we entered the 'twilight zone'? "Well Mike?" I asked hesitantly, trying to decide what to do. The guys who came to pick up Shelly and Lisa didn't seem too pleased with the idea. I got the feeling we were infringing on their territory.

"I don't know," Mike replied, mulling it over in his head.

"Oh, come on. It'll be fun!" they tempted.

"I'll tell you what," I suggested. "Why don't you give us your address and phone number and we'll see. If we don't show, we'll catch you in a few months on our way back home."

"Hope to see ya tonight," Shelly winked after giving us their information. "Or give us a call." With that they locked the doors to the facility, got into their cars and drove off, leaving us alone, standing out front with our bicycles and our thoughts. We got out a map to see where they lived. It would require a side-trip out of our way.

"What are you thinking?" I asked Mike.

"It might be fun, but it doesn't feel right."

"You're right, it doesn't feel right. But what about my dream? In it we got asked to a party. And the pool being here. It's too spooky. I'm not superstitious but… it seemed so real. Maybe we should go to their party simply to thwart my dream. What could it hurt? Dude, I don't want you dead."

"Enough with this dead stuff. You're creeping me out."

"Well?"

"Okay, let's go to the party," Mike consented. "This is all so crazy. Maybe it'll be fun. And don't give me this thwart your dream bull, it's those two cuties you're really thinking about."

An hour later we reached Shelly's home. You could already hear the music blaring from outside. I looked at Mike. He looked back at me hesitantly, seeming to reconsider our decision to come. "We're here," I said.

"Yes, we are here," Mike repeated. "But let's not hang out too long and overstay our welcome."

"Sounds like a good idea," I responded as I knocked on the front door.

Shelly, our alluring winker friend from the pool, answered. "Come on in," she greeted cheerfully, "I knew you'd make it." I got the feeling she usually got what she wanted. She grabbed my hand and led me into the house.

"Will our bikes be okay parked outside?"

"We'll just put them right inside the door here," she offered. "That way you won't have to worry about them."

We worked our way through a maze of people and then into the back room where a bunch of them were dancing. "Would you like something to drink?" she asked.

"I don't know. What do you have?" I answered. I looked over at Mike. Lisa, our other new friend, already had her arm around him. 'Awfully friendly,' I thought.

"There's a keg out on the patio."

"I guess I'll have a beer then, but what about your parents?" I questioned.

"Oh, they don't care. They let us do this all the time, just so long as we don't tear up the house."

"Wow! Your parents sure are permissive." I commented.

With that we headed out onto the patio. Mike and Lisa joined us. After we all downed a cold beer, Lisa asked Mike if he wanted to dance. Mike looked at me and I knew what he was thinking. What about our girlfriends back home? I simply shrugged my shoulders in resignation and we all headed back inside. We really enjoyed the dancing as they were playing some of our favorite songs from Three Dog Night and Chicago. The tempo, which had been really hopping, switched to a slow song. Shelly looked into my eyes. Hers told me to wrap my arms around her. Let's dance, they said. How could I refuse? I didn't want to disappoint her. Evidently, my buddy didn't want to upset Lisa either. They already had their arms entangled around each other and were grooving to the music. Shelly rested her head on my shoulder, pulling her body close to mine while we danced. I looked across the room and red flags jumped up in my head. They were flapping wildly. DANGER! DANGER! Several guys were watching us carefully with the 'if-looks-could-kill, you'd-be-dead' kind of stares.

Dancing with Shelly, I slowly worked my way across the floor towards Mike and Lisa. "Psst," I whispered to Mike. "Those guys over there don't look too happy with us."

Mike glanced over at them. "Yeah, they don't, do they? Maybe we should leave."

"I think that's a good idea. It's been fun, but it's time to go."

Shelly and Lisa protested. "Don't worry about those guys," they said. "They're harmless."

Just the same, Mike and I didn't feel comfortable. We felt the need to leave. We both went to give the girls good-bye kisses, on their cheeks, but they wouldn't have it. They wanted more. It was almost simultaneous instant lip lock. OOPS! Not good. What may have been trophy kisses for the girls looked to be a war cry for the guys. Their cauldron seemed to have really gotten stirred up now. Mike and I didn't waste any time retrieving our bikes, saying good-bye, and quickly pedaling our way out of there.

"Well Mike, wha'da'ya think?" I asked.

"She was a good kisser."

"Not that you idiot. You know what I mean."

"All I know is that we were out-numbered. I sure didn't feel like a fight."

"Me neither," I agreed, "and they'd definitely been drinking for some time."

We went back to the main highway heading north. It felt good to be riding again. It was still warm, but it was a comfortable warm, unlike the furnace we were riding in earlier. We decided to keep on riding into the night until we tired or found an exceptionally good spot to camp. It was easy pedaling, with little traffic and flat terrain.

We pedaled on and on. All we could see on this country road was what our headlights lit up. Looking off to the side wasn't much use as we could only barely see the dark form of what appeared to be a tree or a bush. Occasionally, we heard that eerie sound of an oil pump, forever turning, drawing up the liquid gold from underground. They never tired and worked on and on. Only a few vehicles passed us. Lights would come up from behind, get brighter and brighter, and then WHooSH! We'd be cast back into darkness, watching taillights fade off into the distance. We continued pedaling.

"Mike, how you feeling?" It was almost 9:30pm.

"I'm getting a little tired. How 'bout you?"

"I'm getting there too. You want to find a place to camp for the night?"

"Yeah, let's check our map."

We pulled over to the side of the road, got out a flashlight and our map, and determined where the next town was. It was about 15 to 20 miles away which would take us about another hour to ride. This was going to be our next stop.

We continued our pedaling. It was a peaceful night. Stars were scattered in the sky above. Few words were exchanged. The sound of our breathing seemed amplified in the quiet. For the first time this night some lights came at us head-on. They got brighter and brighter, nearly blinding us, and then WHoooSh! A big truck went by. Its tailwind hit us square in the face, slowing us down to a crawl. Mike and I didn't care for that one bit. It made us appreciate the few trucks that came from behind, whose lights did not blind us, and whose tailwinds actually helped push us along. This must have been the busy time of night because a few minutes later some more lights closed in on us from behind. It sure was much nicer than coming from head-on. They got brighter and brighter and *SMACK!* I no sooner looked back over my shoulder to see what happened to Mike and *SMACK!!* I got clobbered too. 'What the...,' I thought as I went tumbling off my bicycle and into the ditch on the side of the road. I just missed rolling into the irrigation water. My arms felt scraped up and achy but nothing seemed broken. I quickly got to my feet. "Mike, Mike, you all right?" I yelled back to my buddy. There was no answer. "Mike..."

"I'm all right," he finally replied unsteadily. "My head hurts. I think I'm bleeding. What was that all about?" Mike asked. He also had been knocked off his bicycle, only his head had hit the asphalt road.

"You need a doctor?" I asked.

"No, I'll be okay."

"How do you know you're okay? You can't even see yourself."

"Trust me, I'm okay. Okay?"

"Okay."

Moments later we heard the screeching of tires and then saw a pair of headlights leering at us from down the road. There was the sound of glass bottles breaking. A car sat there revving its engine as if to torment us. It was doing a good job of it. Running wasn't an option. We had all our stuff and there was this irrigation ditch alongside the road.

"I'll bet they're the guys from that party," Mike guessed.

"You oughta be a brain surgeon," I replied sarcastically. "I don't know how many of them there are, but be smart, they've been drinking. And if you're going down, take someone with you."

"What do you mean if I'm going down? It wasn't my idea to go to that party."

"It could be worse. At least you didn't end up under a car."

"So far. You and your dream."

The driver gunned the engine of the car, its tires squealed, then it came racing towards us. "Get ready, here they come, " I warned.

"No kidding Sherlock. What gave you that clue?" The tension mounted. It was fight or flight time and we weren't going anywhere. Adrenalin coursed through our veins.

As the car neared, we heard its engine rapidly downshifting until it came to a stop on the road next to us. Its windows were all down. Sure enough, it was them. The driver laughed. It was an evil, up-to-no-good laugh. One of the thugs hung out the rear window. He flipped open a switchblade. Waving the knife back and forth, its blade flashing in the moonlight, he shouted out, "Them's our girls. Stay away from 'em,… get the point?"

"We get the point," Mike answered. "We're leaving."

The driver, who had a nasty scar on his face, added, "We don't want to see you again." After quickly guzzling a beer he tossed the empty bottle out his window. It shattered on the roadway. He screamed in delight, floored the gas pedal, and burned rubber, his tires again squealing, trying to grab the asphalt. Finally the tires took hold, and the car, with its hoodlums, went speeding back towards town. All that remained was dust and the stench of burnt rubber.

"Whew! We dodged a bullet there," I exclaimed.

"We sure did," Mike sighed in relief. "Let's not do that again."

"Agreed. You know what's really cool?" I asked.

"No, what?"

"You're not dead, and I'm not paralyzed. How cool is that?"

"Way cool. Now can we get off this dead and paralyzed nonsense you're tripping on?"

"Tripping? Wait'll I tell you about my hallucinations from the drugs they had me taking at the hospital. There was…"

"Enough already," Mike groaned in exasperation. "Let's get riding. In less than an hour we can be at our next stop for the night." With that, we dusted ourselves off, gathered our gear back together, and rode on. Wasco was the next town. And that name rhymes with fiasco. Wasco, fiasco. What lurked ahead?

Chapter Three

Strip Tease

When we awoke on the 8th of August...Stop! Did you notice the pronoun we? That infers both Mike and me. Yes, we were still alive, both of us. Mike hadn't been run over and killed by a drunk driver, and I wasn't in a Bakersfield hospital, paralyzed and on a respirator fighting for my life. Came close maybe, but didn't happen. That had been one wild dream. I got out a pen and some paper my girlfriend Shari had given me to keep in touch and began writing about my dream. 'Gee, if I write a little every day,' I thought, 'I could have enough for a whole book by the time we get back home.' I decided to send Shari what I'd written each day along with a postcard detailing our trip. It would help keep Shari happy, feeling connected and all.

"Hey, Mike, you up?" I asked.

"Yep," he answered.

"It's a beautiful day in the neighborhood."

"Are you hallucinating?"

"Glad you brought that up. You ready to hear about one of my hallucinations?" I asked eagerly.

"Not now, I gotta check out my face, it's hurtin'."

"I could have told you that years ago. How else were you going to land such a looker like Colleen. She felt sorry for you."

"Oh yeah, that's what Shari told me about you. We must be related."

"Okay, come here. Let's see that ugly mug of yours." Mike walked towards me. "Ouch!" I winced as I saw the damage.

"That bad?"

"Ain't pretty. Dude, you have to stop doing superman imitations off your bike." I got out our first-aid kit and cleaned the dried blood off Mike's face. "Not much of an improvement," I quipped. "You're just as ugly as ever."

"Very funny, he replied. "Let's not mention this to Colleen or Shari, they'd freak out."

"Agreed. Moms either, at least not 'til we're safely back home."

A little northeast of where we were was Kings Canyon National Park. I told Mike about the bike trip I'd taken with my good friend Brett a year earlier. On that trip we did the long gnarly mountain climb in to that park. It took a grueling six and a half hours of uphill pedaling to reach the top. On the way up Brett sprained all of his fingers from pulling so hard on his handlebars and my legs kept cramping the last couple miles of that trek. It was a very physically demanding ride, but a breathtakingly beautiful one and well worth the effort. Mike's interest was piqued. He insisted on having a go at it. Side trip here we come.

We rode that day north and east, through Visalia, and then found a small campground to stay at near the base of the mountain. It had been easy riding. That was a good thing because I knew we were going to be expending a whole lot of energy pedaling up the beast the next day. We got a crackling campfire started and were going to hit the hay early, but first...

"Mike, you ready?" I asked.

"Ready for what?" he replied.

"For one of my hallucinations."

"Oh, do I have to?" he whined. "Just kidding! Let's hear what your warped mind dreamed up."

"Come to think of it, I am kinda tired and we do need our sleep. I'll tell you about it tomorrow."

"Dude, you just messin' with me? You're not really going to leave me hanging, are you?"

I rolled over in my sleeping bag. "Tomorrow, Mike, I'll tell you about it tomorrow."

"That ain't right," Mike protested.

Soon after, we were both sound asleep.

The next morning Mike was up early. "Okay, let's have it," he said. "Have what?" I answered as I sat up in my sleeping bag.

"You know, your hallucination."

"'Actually, there was more than one. Kinda got you wondering about them now, hey, little buddy?" I kidded.

"Little buddy," Mike chaffed. "You cruisin' for a bruisin'?"

"You are an inch or two shorter than me," I pointed out. "I'm just teasing. You know me. I'll tell you what. It'll be hard, but from now on I'll try and refrain myself,   ...a little." I grinned. "Ain't promising anything though."

"Okay BIG buddy. Now how about the hallucination?"

"Can't. I lost my train of thought. I'll tell you one of them when we reach the summit. There's a log cabin country restaurant up there where we can eat. I guarantee you that by the time we get there we'll be plenty hungry and ready for a good break. For now, there's a place for breakfast just a short distance from here."

It was a bit farther than I remembered. We found the quaint little inn tucked off to the side, shaded by dense forest. A small stream flowed behind it. This certainly was gorgeous country! After parking our bicycles we went in to get something to eat. The same two window seats that Brett and I had on my previous trip were available. We sat down in them and placed our order.

"Check out those hummingbirds," I commented. There were two feeders hanging right outside our window.

"One of God's amazing creations," Mike pointed out.

"Sure are," I agreed. "And get a load of that."

"Of what?"

"That bird hovering there. He's the same bird I saw here on my last trip."

"No way! That was over a year ago. How could you know?"

"It's easy. He has the same yellow markings, and,..." I paused.

"And what?"

"...and, he winked at me."

Mike quickly turned towards our waitress. "Excuse me," he interrupted. "Is our breakfast about ready yet? I think my friend here is getting delusional."

Pancakes, hash-brown potatoes, bacon, and eggs were served. We gobbled that up, washed it all down with a large glass of orange juice, and were energized and ready for our ascent. Mike and I had started out the day near sea level in elevation. A lengthy skyward climb now lie ahead. We stretched for a few minutes, then resumed our ride. I'm thinking the word ride sounds too soft, like we're going for a ride in a car, you know, leisurely, without much, if any effort at all. I knew it was far from that.

We reached the entrance to the park which was at 1,200 feet in elevation. How steep and nasty was the upcoming road from there going to be? It was so difficult that the young ranger-lady was advising all campers longer than 22 feet not to attempt it. This wasn't a problem for us. She then asked us why we wanted to do this and if we really thought we'd enjoy ourselves. I think she thought we were nuts, operating without all our eggs in one basket. We simply told her we loved the challenge and left her with five little words: "'See you at the top!'"

Off we pedaled, pedaling steadily uphill the 18 miles it took to get to the Giant Forest. The climb was just like I remembered — a cardio-pumping, muscle-taxing, energy-sapping test of endurance. It was a long and mentally draining battle, especially the last hour as we neared our goal. You'd think you were at the top, and then 'UGH!', there'd be another rise around the next bend. This happened repeatedly, turn after turn, rise after rise, like one skirmish after another. It had become all out war, us against the mountain. And then, just when it seemed like we'd never get there, we arrived!!

Shoot off the fireworks! Raise the victory flag! After six tortuous hours, we reached the lodge in Giant Forest, elevation 6,700 feet. That's 5,500 feet higher than at the park entrance. That's over one mile straight up! Two weary riders got off their bicycles and with wobbly legs walked in to get something to eat. We were famished. It was chow down time. No sooner had we gotten seated when in walked the ranger from this morning. She spotted us.

"Look at this. You two sure made it up here in record time. You get a lift?" she grinned.

"Nope. Pedal power, and lots of perspiration," Mike answered proudly.

"I've only got a few minutes, but do you mind if I join you?" she asked.

"Not at all, have a seat," I replied. She sat down and removed her ranger's hat. Long sandy-blonde hair spilled out, cascading down her neck and over her shoulders. It was like a spectacular waterfall. Her blue eyes sparkled. Yowser! She was stunning. "You are the prettiest ranger I have ever seen," I complimented.

"And how many rangers is that?" she smiled broadly. And I'll tell you, her smile could light up a dark cavernous room.

"Well, not many. But if you were in a room with a thousand other rangers, I'd bet you'd be the prettiest one there."

"You're just being kind."

"No, I'm serious," I said emphatically, while trying to appear unrattled by her beauty.

Mike chuckled. "Sounds like my buddy, excuse me, my BIG buddy, wouldn't mind being Yogi Bear if he could live in your park."

"Big buddy?" Sandy questioned.

"He is an inch taller than I am."

With that we all laughed. The three of us chatted for a bit before our new-found ranger friend said she had to get back to work. She stood up and re-tucked her hair back into her hat while putting it on. Then came the proposal, one that sounded awfully familiar...

"Why don't you two come to a party I'm having tonight?"

"And where might that be?" I asked.

"At my place in Fresno. It's on your way, and it'll be lots of fun!"

Mike gave me the 'we're not going to do this again' look before I answered, "Sounds good to me, but we don't even know your name."

"It's Sandra. There, now you know me. Will you come? There'll be plenty of food and drinks."

'Sandra, sandy blonde hair,' I thought. "Do you mind if I call you Sandy?"

"No, all my friends do."

Thinking that I'd love to be her friend, I then said, "Sandy, give us your address and phone number and we'll see."

Sandy wrote down the info and then said with an air of confidence, "See you tonight." She looked back over her shoulder one last time as she exited and flashed a very enticing smile.

"Well, Mike? What do you think?"

"I think we're going to get ourselves shot or skewered. Get the point!"

"Is that a yes or a no?" I asked.

"I'll tell you, it goes against my better judgment, but if you want we can go. It's obvious you're dyin' to see blondie again."

We finished our hearty lunch, and then went back outside. It was an awesome setting. Sky-scraping Giant Sequoias reached for the heavens. An angelic light filtered through their branches. The splendor and enormity of God's creation really hit us as we gazed upward. Sugar and ponderosa pines also filled the mountainsides. This forest was quite amazing. While we stood there, taking it all in, Mike remembered something.

"Hey, what about your hallucination? We're here."

"Oh, yeah, I guess we got distracted by the ranger."

"We?" Mike disagreed. "You're the one under blondie's spell."

"Okay, which one should I tell you?"

"I don't know. You tell me."

"All right, here goes. I was in the hospital barracks and in walked this pudgy... no, wait, I'll tell you a different one. I was in bed in a hospital room when my nurse told me not to go up into the attic... no, wait. First I'll tell you the bird one. I was ..."

"Stop already! You're still tryin' to drive me crazy, aren't you? I know the air is thin at this elevation, but come on, this is insane. Take a deep breath and let's get back to the pudgy one. Don't make me wish I'd gotten run over back there in Bakersfield."

I grinned. "Okay. I was in some hospital barracks when in walked this pudgy middle-aged nurse. She had a coarse, no-nonsense air about her as she matter-of-factly spouted out, 'We have to graft some skin off your arm'. So, being as trusting as I was, and thinking that surely she must know what she's doing, I never even questioned her. At least not until she pulled out a long piece of nylon thread. I asked her what it was for. She smiled and told me she was going to use it to cut into my skin. Saves money and it's much easier, she said. I chuckled and told her she's got to be kidding, knowing that she must be joking with me. You know me, I'm a bit of a practical joker myself. My motto is: Don't take life too seriously, nobody gets out alive."

Mike agreed, "Yeah, you are a bit of a quack-up."

I continued, "Just about then, another nurse, stockier than the first, walked in to my room. She came right over to me, forcefully grabbed my arm, and pinned it down to my bed. Then the first dastardly nurse began sawing feverishly into my arm with the thread. It was too bizarre and happening so fast. I was freaked! 'What are you doing?!' I demanded. 'Stop! This isn't right!' I was helpless. The nurse acted like she didn't hear me and continued sawing back and forth, cutting deep into my skin. She seemed oblivious to my loud protests. 'These must be a couple of loony-bird nurses, straight out of an asylum,' I thought. *SPLAAT!!* Blood hit the ceiling and was squirting all over the place. 'Geez!' I thought. 'She must have hit an artery.'"

"Dude, you were really trippin'," Mike laughed.

"I tell you, Mike, it seemed so real. It was like this really happened to me. Then, as quickly as it happened, it was over. The nurses left. I was feeling quite weak. It was strange, but everything seemed to be all right again. I was still alive, drained, but alive. Then I drifted back off to sleep."

Mike was fascinated. I wanted to show him the scars on my arm but of course there weren't any. That's how real it seemed. We talked a bit more about my dream and hallucinations, and then hit the road. A little farther ahead we stopped at the General Sherman tree for a picture. Standing beside this gigantic Sequoia made us feel so insignificant. It's thought to be the largest tree in the world, which probably makes it the largest living thing on planet Earth. It stands about 275 feet tall and is about 103 feet around at its base. That's humungous!

From there, we continued our ride through the rest of King's Canyon. As we started our descent, zig-zagging down the curvy mountain road, I warned Mike about following too closely behind slower moving motor homes and campers. I knew from past experience what could happen. On my last trip with Brett, I had been right on the tail of a camper, waiting for an opportunity to pass him on one of the next turns. I was doing about 25 mph. Suddenly, a small pothole appeared right in front of me. There was no time to react. All I could do was hang on for dear life. Both tires struck it, throwing me and my bicycle up into the air. It scared the crap out of me! Fortunately, I landed safely, with no injuries, and no blown tires. Let's call it dumb luck, a lesson learned.

Evidently, my warning didn't make much of an impression on Mike, because there he was, right on the tail of a camper. I followed at a safe distance and watched. Sure enough, he too hit a pothole. Unlike me, he went flying over his handlebars and onto the roadway, repeating his caped crusader imitation from the other night. It was scary! I quickly stopped to help.

"Mike, are you all right? You idiot, I told you not to tailgate!"

"I'm okay," Mike responded. "How's my bike?"

"Your bike looks fine, no flats or anything, but you better watch it. Keep this up and you're gonna get yourself killed!"

"Then no party tonight, no goldilocks, hey? I'll bet that's your main concern."

"Oh yeah. Well, look who's the one in such a hurry to get there. Take it easy."

At a more leisurely speed, we traversed down the rest of the mountain. The road leveled off and we headed on to Fresno. One good-looking ranger lady, and who knows what else, awaited.

It was dark by the time we hit Fresno. We found a pay phone, put a dime in the slot, and made the call. Sandy answered and gave us directions to her place. She sounded overly excited that we were coming. What's up with that, we wondered? She barely knew us. Soon we'd be finding out. It was just a short jaunt to her house from there.

"Mike, you ready?" I asked while standing on their doorstep.

"Ready for what?" he responded, "I'm going to be ticked off if we're dodging gunfire leaving this place."

"Who knows?!" I knocked. Sandy answered.

"Hi. I'm so glad you two came," she smiled. "Come on in and meet my friends."

We brought our bikes right inside the door, looked around, and lo and behold, only three other girls were there, no guys. Mike and I exchanged quizzical looks.

"Is this everybody?" I asked.

"Oh, did I forget to mention it's just a small party with a few of my girlfriends?" Sandy replied. "We're playing cards."

"I guess you did forget to mention that," I answered.

"You do play cards, don't you?"

"We do," I said. Mike nodded his head in agreement.

"Then have a seat. Can I get you a beer and some chips?"

"Sure. We'll have whatever you're having." We sat down at the table and introduced ourselves to her friends. They were as good-looking as she was. 'This could be an interesting evening,' I thought.

"What kind of cards are you playing?" Mike questioned.

Sandy answered, "Poker. Do you know how to play?"

"Yes," we said in unison.

"Any good?"

"Not bad," Mike responded. I agreed.

"Now that you guys are here we thought it would be fun to play a special type of poker."

"Oh yeah, what's that?" we asked.

"Strip poker. Have you ever played it?" Sandy asked. The other three girls all giggled giddily.

I looked at Mike, and Mike's eyes got big. "Did I hear you right? You did say strip poker, didn't you?"

"Yes, I did say strip poker. You do know how to play, don't you?"

I'm thinking, she can't mean strip poker like the strip poker I'm thinking. That would be too absurd. So to clarify the situation, I asked, "And just how do you play strip poker?"

"Are you kidding me?" Sandy answered.

"No, I'm just curious. Maybe you play a different version."

"Didn't know there was one. It's quite simple. You know, you lose a hand, you have to take off a piece of clothing. It's fun! It's exciting!"

I looked at Mike, and Mike's eyes were really big now, like saucers. 'What kind of a mess are we getting ourselves into now?' I thought.

"You all want to play this?" I asked, looking around at the others in disbelief.

They all kept smiling and said, yes, they were in. Then Sandy asked, "Are you guys in, or are you too scared to play? You're not chicken, are you?" She shuffled the cards. And she was no rookie at card shuffling.

Again, I looked at Mike. "Mike, you chicken?" Mike looked awfully skittish.

"No," he said hesitantly. "You chicken?"

Dang, this was extremely awkward! But I sure didn't want to be a chicken either. I looked at the four of them and they all still kept smiling.

One of Sandy's friends then asked, "You guys aren't scared to take your clothes off, are you?"

"No, we're not scared," I replied. "And it seems like you're not too concerned about stripping down either. I doubt we'd be losing anyway. Truth is, we simply haven't come across a situation like this before. This just isn't the typical kind of party we get invited to."

Then, unable to contain herself any longer, Sandy busted out laughing, and the three of them with her. "Gotcha! We're just teasing you."

There was a collective sigh of relief between Mike and me. Too weird. But I couldn't let it end there.

"Are you kidding me?" I said, seeming disappointed. "I was starting to look forward to a wild and crazy poker game. I'm sure Mike was too." Mike kicked me under the table but I went on. "Don't tell me you beautiful young ladies are all chicken. You're not scared to show us what you've got, are you?" Mike kicked me again.

We played poker long into the night, regular poker that is, with clothes on. And we ate. And we drank. And we had a great time. Names and numbers were exchanged in the hope that our paths would cross again. Perhaps they would on our return trip. I loved the idea. I hadn't shared with Mike yet the troubling thoughts I was having about Sheri and me. Could Sandy be in my future? Mike and I slept on her couches that night.

Chapter Four

Rolling Stone

The next morning we thanked Sandy and her roommate for their hospitality, then bicycled off north towards Sacramento. It was already quite hot out by the time we got underway. As we left Fresno we rode through the San Joaquin Valley, a region with over a million acres of farmland. We passed fields of oranges, grapes and cotton along the way. After a few hours we came upon the small town of Chowchilla, an Indian name which translates to 'murderers'. It's named after the Chauchila Indians, a tribe known for their warlike nature. Yosemite Valley was discovered when white men pursued them up into the mountains just east of there. During the months of preparation for our trip, Mike and I had done a lot of research on our planned route and the towns we'd come upon. We wanted to to get a feel for their history as we traveled through them. Actually seeing these places was intriguing. It was like transporting ourselves back into the pages of time.

While we rode Mike had a thought-provoking question for me. His inquiring mind was dying to know. "Would you really have played strip poker back there or were you bluffing?" he asked.

"Well, little buddy, you got to know when to hold 'em, know when to fold 'em. You got to know when to walk away, know when to run. Gee, I think I'm on to what could have the makings of a killer song. What do you think?"

"Very funny. How 'bout just answering my question?"

"I guess we'll never know. Unless the situation really came about, how am I to know what I would've done?"

"Oh, come on, you know," Mike pushed.

"Maybe, … but then again, maybe not."

"Sometimes you can be so exasperating."

"That's a ten dollar word."

"Well, are you going to tell me?"

"It's a mystery." I grinned.

An hour and a half later, after Chowchilla, we reached Merced, the Western Gateway to the Yosemite National Park. From there we came to Turlock. Agriculture and cattle-ranching are the engines that keep this town running. It used to be known for having the most churches per person, the reason being that it had such diverse groups of people living there. It was still a blistering hot day as we continued cycling. Mike and I stayed hydrated by drinking lots of water and occasionally snatching an orange off of a low-hanging tree branch. Evening had arrived by the time we reached our final destination for the day, Modesto. It's a railroad-stop type town whose name was derived from folklore. It's said that the people of this town wanted to name it after an influential banker, but he did not want his name used. A Spanish railroad worker then commented that he was "muy modesto" — very modest — and thus the name came about.

Mike and I got out our sleeping bags and were beginning to relax in a park by the railroad tracks when two young ladies approached. Dismayed, Mike looked over at me, "Here we go again."

"Mike, you can't help yourself, you just have that animal magnetism about you."

"You mean, like a bee is attracted to a flower?"

"No, I was thinking more like a dog's attracted to a fire hydrant."

The girls neared. "Are you guys hungry?" one of them asked.

"A little," I said. "We've been riding all day."

"Are you two hobos?" she continued.

"Oh, no!" Mike exclaimed, embarrassed by that label. "My friend here just looks like one. I know he's unkempt. He's a bum. He hasn't taken the time to wash up or comb his hair. What's it been, a week now?" he teased.

"Very funny. My buddy here is working on becoming a comedian."

"Good for him," the other girl said. "Are you going to be his sidekick?"

"He's going to get a kick all right, right in his hindquarters. Actually, we're on a cross-country bicycle trip. We're on our way to Minnesota."

"How interesting," she replied, but not really seeming to care. "We're from St. Mary's and we're trying to help hungry homeless people. We'll leave you with a couple of drinks and some rolls to munch on. Good luck on your journey. May God be with you." And bango, just like that, they walked off. There was no party invitation this time.

Mike laughed, "Looks like you're a real chick magnet yourself. They sure didn't stay long."

The sound of trains coming and going became hypnotizing once we got used to it. It made for a very deep, restive night's sleep.

The next morning we again packed and checked the area to make sure we weren't leaving anything behind. After a brisk early morning ride, we reached Manteca, another agricultural town. It's called the 'Family City' because it lies at a crossroads of major highways and railroads. A short time later we pedaled into Stockton, founded in 1848 by a German gold-miner who discovered that serving the needs of gold-miners was much more profitable for him than the actual gold-mining. Named after Commodore Robert Stockton, it was the first city in California to not be named after a Spanish or Indian name. From there, with the sun now blazing down upon us again, we came to Lodi, a town known for its wine-making. It's often referred to as the "Zinfandel Capital of the world." Being underage, we weren't able to sample the goods. Lodi also has historical links with the Gold Rush and Sutter's Fort. Captain John Sutter had obtained a land grant along the Sacramento River and one of his foremen discovered gold there. It launched one of the most colorful eras in California's history.

After Lodi, we rode a couple hours more and came to Sacramento, our state's capital. Where was the motorcade to usher us into the city?

Where was the parade, the pomp and circumstance? Didn't they get what we were accomplishing? I guess not. There was no honorary key to the city awaiting us. It was simply another day, business as usual. During the California Gold Rush days, Sacramento was the center for transportation. Wagon trains, the Pony Express, the first transcontinental railroad, stagecoaches, and riverboats were all coming and going. It was a city on the move. Words even traveled at the telegraph office. We spent several hours walking around the capital taking in some of its history, then headed outside of town to find a place to camp for the night.

The following day, thirty miles north of Sacramento, we came upon yet another small Gold Rush town called Marysville. It's named after Mary Murphy Covillaud, one of the surviving members of the Donner Party. The Donner Party consisted of a group of American immigrants caught up in the "Go-West" fever of the 1840s. Most of the settlers that had been part of that large wagon train died on the way. It had been an extremely harsh journey, plagued with bad weather. At one point, the group became snow-bound, whereupon they even had to resort to cannibalism.

"I'm starving. Let's get something to eat," Mike grimaced, his stomach growling loudly.

"Hey dude, don't be lookin' at me that way," I replied. "This reminds me of another one of those hallucinations from my dream."

"Another hallucination, eh? When do I get to hear this one?"

"How about now?"

"Shoot."

"Bang! There I was in the hospital barracks, just lying there minding my own business, when this nurse walks up to me and tells me to stay out of the attic. I thought, 'yeah, right, like I'm gonna go up in an attic. I didn't even know there was one.' Then, across from me on the wall, I noticed rungs leading up to a ledge and an attic door. 'Oh crap!' I thought, 'Why'd she have to tell me that? Now my mind longs to know what's up there.'"

"So what was up there?" Mike asked.

"I don't know. I didn't go."

"No way, you'd have climbed those rungs. I know you better than that."

"You're right, I did climb those rungs, got on to the ledge, and then flung open the attic door. It was like a gigantic airplane hangar inside. An icy cold draft chilled me as I peered into the darkness. Then, through the faint shadowy light, I noticed something flashing in the distance. It seemed to be approaching at a rapid pace. When my eyes finally adjusted to the dark, there it was, a huge saber-toothed tiger. He was closing in on me quickly and had that ravenous, 'I know what's for dinner' look in his eyes. In utter panic, I slammed the attic door shut and quickly began backing down the rungs. My heart racing, in a tizzy, I got dizzy and froze up. I couldn't move. Everything was swirling about me. Pale-faced patients gathered below and stared up at me. Their ghoulish stares were empty, devoid of emotion, like a bunch of zombies. Finally, the nurse that told me not to go into the attic rescued me. She was furious. I got a fire-breathing dragon-like tongue lashing from her and was then escorted back to bed. I'll tell you, that hospital was a house of horrors."

"Sounds like it," Mike agreed. "That was one weird hallucination."

"Sure was, and the funny thing is, like before, it felt so real."

We were getting closer to my cousin Chuck's house, Mike's brother. Soon he and his wife, Sue, would be getting an earful about our exciting journey thus far. But first we had to ride through Oroville, a town founded back in the 1850s when a group of Cherokee Indians migrated there from Georgia. Diamonds were discovered in a nearby town called Cherokee. Could good fortune be beckoning us? We couldn't resist that notion and took the little side trip. It ended in a virtual ghost town. What we saw, the ruins of brick stores, is pretty much all that remained. No dazzling stones were found.

Only nine miles stood between us and Chico, our first major stop on this trip. It was going to be a fun visit with Chuck and Sue, newlyweds attending school at Chico State. Chico is more of a college town now but it had been known for its many orchards. Row after row after row of almond, walnut, and cherry trees lined the countryside like lines on college-ruled notebook paper. In 1843 General John Bidwell founded Chico after coming across America on one of the first wagon trains to reach the West. He was a leading nineteenth-century agriculturalist. Mike and I were going to spend a whole week here. The week was planned to include some inner-tubing down the Sacramento River and some backpacking at nearby Mt. Shasta.

As we neared my cousin's house, his dog, a big German Shepherd, came running to greet us. Mike and I jumped off our bicycles.

"Duke, how ya doing ol' boy?" I asked.

"Woof, woof, woof," he replied.

"You miss us?" Mike added.

"Woof, woof, woof," he answered again.

Duke didn't have much of a vocabulary, but his body language spoke volumes. His tail was a wagging a mile-a-minute, he was barking loudly, and he was running excitedly back and forth between us. Then he went and fetched a rock and set it at my feet. He backed up a couple of steps, sat down, and looked up at me expectantly.

"What'cha want ol' boy?" I teased.

Duke walked forward impatiently and nudged the rock with his nose. He returned to sitting and again looked up at me. He began whimpering and then let out two sharp urgent yelps, like "stop messing with me, you know what I want." I knew. I'd taken care of Duke before. Earlier that summer Mike and I spent a lot of time throwing rocks for him to fetch. To Duke's extreme delight, I picked up the rock and tossed it across the yard. He took off after it like a bat out of hell, his legs scampering as fast as they could go. Having retrieved the rock, this time he set it at Mike's feet. Mike picked up the rock and...

"No! No! No!" Chuck yelled running out his front door, "Not that! We're trying to break him of that habit."

"We're glad to see you too," Mike kidded.

"Yeah, what kind'a welcome is that?" I threw in.

"I'm glad to see you guys, but the rocks, they're doing a number on Duke's teeth. We took him to the vet the other day and he told us that they were a mess."

"You sure it's the rocks? Maybe he hasn't been flossing after meals," I quipped.

About then Sue came out of the house. "Hi, boys, I thought I heard you out here." She gave us each a warm hug. "You must be starving. Would you like something to eat?"

"Does Duke like to fetch rocks?" I answered. Sue looked at Chuck with a 'what are we going to do with this guy' kind of look. And I quickly continued, "The answer is yes. And I'm really sorry about Duke's teeth. I feel partly responsible."

"Good," Chuck smiled. "Then you can help pay for his dentures."

"His dentures?!"

"Just kidding. But no more rocks! They really are ruining his teeth."

I squatted down and scratched Duke on the back of his head. "Sorry ol' boy. It's rubber duckies for you, no more hard stuff."

We went in and spent the rest of the day grazing on food. Sue was a wonderful hostess. While we were sitting around enjoying a few brewskies with Chuck, he informed us that he didn't think the Mt. Shasta climb we'd planned on was such a good idea. Sure, there'd been a near record amount of snowfall that past winter, but even so, by this time of year the icepack had thinned out. This creates problems with rock fall, even possible avalanches. And then, he hypothesized, there could be a problem with the Lemurians.

This drew a big "what the heck is a Lemurian?" from the two of us.

Chuck went on to explain that the Lemurians are a highly intelligent civilization from the lost continent of Lemuria. Some ten thousand years ago, their continent, which was off the west coast of North America, sank down into the Pacific Ocean. Realizing that imminent disaster and destruction were upon them, they'd built a large city deep inside Mt. Shasta. The city has circular apartments made with gold and is all lit up by one great light over its center. The people who live there are over seven feet tall. They are a graceful and agile people who wear long flowing white robes and sandals on their feet. They have big heads, large foreheads, and long necks. And then came the most extraordinary thing Chuck said about them. He told us that they'd developed the capacity to communicate with each other using mental telepathy and that they can transport themselves back and forth between the material world and the spiritual world. Rarely though, has one been seen traveling in and out of the mountain.

Chuck continued his expose. He told us that Mt. Shasta had a real spiritual mystique about it. That many New Agers selling crystals and such had set up shop around there. He said that the mountain, which could be seen a hundred miles away on a clear day, oftentimes had its majestic peak shrouded in mystical cloud formations. That nearby Native Indian tribes believed that during creation, the "Great Spirit" used it as a stepping stone when descending from heaven to create life on this planet.

All Chuck did was create more of a desire to conquer this 14,162 foot wonder.

"So what's the big deal about the Lemurians?" Mike asked. "They sound like nice people."

"They are nice, and peaceful, but can you imagine having hordes of people climbing on your roof. It's my theory that the Lemurians cause some of that rock-fall I'd like to avoid. I think they do it in an effort to reduce traffic on their mountain, to preserve its integrity and give themselves some rest."

"Sounds reasonable to me," Mike said, acknowledging Chuck's response.

"Whoa, wait a minute!" I exclaimed incredulously. "You guys don't for a second believe this stuff?" About then I noticed a sizeable crystal on a shelf on the wall. Sue saw me looking at it.

"That's a housewarming gift. A neighbor gave it to us when we first moved in," she explained. "It's just a beautiful rock, nothing more. And don't you worry, we don't really believe this stuff. But we do enjoy the folklore, and sometimes it's simply fun to let your imagination run with it."

"You sounded so serious. It had me wondering there for a bit. Strange area, some kind of hex, who knows? It didn't help that I recently saw the movie 'The Exorcist.'"

"Our heads are all on straight," Chuck laughed.

"I'm glad. I was beginning to think somebody's steering wheel had come off."

"When can we do the climb?" Mike asked.

"Guys, there are no trees above the timberline, just ice and rocks. I know of much better hikes with lots of trees and gorgeous views."

"We still want to do it," I persisted. "Besides, we told our girlfriends we'd get a picture of us at the summit,"

"Now look whose steering wheel's come off. You know, if the weather changes, and it can happen rapidly, that you become a human lightening rod on that barren mountain."

"The weather report calls for clear skies the next few days," Sue interjected.

Chuck glared at his wife. She wasn't helping his cause. "Did you know it's a volcano? It's part of the Pacific Ring of Fire. Fire! Molten lava! Eruptions!"

"When did it last erupt?" I asked. "Chuck, you really don't want to do this, do you?"

"No, I really don't want to do this. And for your information, it last erupted two hundred years ago. It's due. I'll tell you, danger is not my game anymore, been there and done that in Vietnam. I like to do things at a more relaxed pace and without a lot of stress."

"That's fine," Mike said, "Mark and I can climb it by ourselves."

"No, no, no, we're not going there. If something happened to the two of you, your mothers would never forgive me."

"Well, we still want to do the climb," Mike held firm. "We can do another hike with you later this week."

I agreed.

"Okay, enough already. If you guys are so determined, I'll do it," Chuck conceded. "There's no way I'll let you tackle it alone. Be forewarned though, if one of you gets hurt I'm going to kill you! We'll go the day after tomorrow while the weather is still good." He gave another 'thanks' look to Sue and then continued. "Tomorrow we'll rent some headlamps because we'll be starting our climb in the dark, say 4am. We'll also need to get some ice axes, crampons, and a few other items."

"Tampons!" I exclaimed. "What in tarnation do we need tampons for? There aren't any ladies going with us."

"No cuz," Mike cut in, "he said crap-ons. You need something to crap on when you're up there. You're not supposed to leave anything on the mountain. You have to be prepared to take anything, no matter how disgusting, back down the mountain with you. You know the saying, 'Pack it in. Pack it out'."

Mike and I looked at each other and busted out laughing. We knew what crampons were. We'd read about them when researching our trip. They're bearclaw-like attachments that fit onto the bottom of your boots. They help keep you from slipping when climbing on icy, snow-packed glaciers. At least two of us thought the jokes were funny. And at least two of us were looking forward to the upcoming experience. It was going to be a memorable one.

Should we have heeded Chuck's advice? We'd soon find out.

At eight-o'clock the following evening the three of us went to sleep in the back of Chuck's truck. We were at the Bunny Flat trailhead on Mt. Shasta, elevation 6,900 feet. This was going to be the starting point of our climb. At 3am we were awakened by some commotion. Turns out this also happened to be a popular starting point for a number of other mountaineers. We ate a quick breakfast, shouldered our packs, strapped on our headlamps, and at 4am began our ascent.

Our first short rest came at Horse Camp. We'd climbed nearly a thousand feet in elevation. Chuck was staying right with us even though he was the old man in the bunch. He was a whopping ten years older but he was in great shape. The air was crisp. The sky was littered with twinkling stars. This surely was a majestic place.

We continued on our way up the mountain to Helen Lake, elevation 10,443 feet. Trees were no longer with us. All that remained was rock, snow, and ice. We were also able to shed our headlamps as morning had broken, just like the first morning. I felt another song coming on here but needed to concentrate on the climb. The terrain was steep and uneven. At times, it seemed like we were just climbing a giant pile of rocks. It was no wonder that the route we were on was called Avalanche Gulch. Chuck wasn't amused, especially when I told him that one section of this climb was nicknamed, 'The Bowling Alley'. "What are we, three pins waiting to be knocked over?" he quipped.

"Climb, Chuck, climb. Let's not waste any time here to find out," I answered.

From there we headed to a ridge up and over Red Banks. A frigid blast of wind met us at that ridge, nearly turning us into popsicles. *Brrr!!!* It was cold. The last hours of climbing, with crampons on, had taken us up another 3,000 feet. At such a high elevation the air was much thinner. Breathing became a struggle. A weariness was setting in. Chuck again uttered sarcastically, "Are we having fun yet?" Mike was proud of his brother, the old man had kept right up with us.

When we reached the base of Misery Hill, we were revived. Our goal was in sight. As we climbed this grueling adversary, it didn't take any stretch of the imagination to understand how it got its name. It was tough. As we hiked past some smelly sulfur springs, Chuck was quick to remind us that this mountain was alive, that it was indeed a volcano.

There was one last steep three-hundred-foot vertical rise to overcome. It stood between us and victory. We gazed heavenward, drew strength from the Almighty, and powered our way to the top. We made it! We had reached our summit. Our arms shot up in triumph as we danced up and down in celebration. It was euphoric. We had conquered the mountain. We were on top of the world. Pictures were taken and then we simply sat there for the next hour, astonished by the view, and in satisfaction of our quest. Chuck even seemed pleased with the accomplishment. It had been a seven hour summit climb.

The descent was much easier than the ascent. We got to do some glissading, sliding down the icy snow-covered sections on our butts. Occasionally we tried it European style by sliding on our feet standing up. Falls and all, it was a blast! Mike, the daredevil, even tried riding down one slope on his pack using its frame like the skis on a sled. Things were going great. But when we got back down below Red Banks things were about to change. We heard a deep earth-shaking rumbling noise from above. What was going on? The three of us looked back up the mountain and...

"Uh-oh!" Mike exclaimed.

"What the heck!" I yelled out.

"I knew it!" Chuck chastised. "But nooooo, you had to do this for your girlfriends."

Bounding down the mountain was a boulder the size of a VW Bug. It was gargantuan! It must've broken loose from its frozen pedestal. The terrifying thing was that there was no place to hide and we couldn't tell which way to move. The boulder kept changing directions.

Chuck quickly shouted out some instructions. "When you think you know where it's going dive the opposite way, stay low, and cover your head."

The boulder veered to the left, then, almost like it had radar, changed course and was speeding directly at us. Momentarily frozen in fear, we were like three deer staring into the headlights of an oncoming semi.

"God help us!" I cried out as Chuck and I dove to the right and Mike dove to the left.

At about fifty feet above us the boulder bounced onto another large rock and split into two. Now there were two giant halves to deal with. One was heading towards Mike, the other towards Chuck and me. There was no time to react. We all cowered in the face of impending disaster. I was pelted by smaller rocks, rock fragments, and ice as one of the giant halves flew over my head. With my heart beating like crazy, I laid there for a few seconds wondering if the onslaught was over. When all the chaos had settled I scrambled to my feet and breathed a sigh of relief. I was still breathing. Ergo, I was still alive.

"Chuck, you all right?" I hollered.

"Not so loud. I'm right here. I'm all right. How 'bout you?"

"I'm okay. I just got hit by a few little pieces. Where's Mike?"

Looking to the left, there he was, lying face down on some rocks. He was motionless.

"Oh crap! Mike, are you all right?" Chuck shouted dreadfully as both he and I ran to him.

Mike didn't respond.

"Mike, say something," I pleaded.

He moved.

"Thank God! You're not dead." My momentarily crushed spirit had new life.

Mike rolled over and sat up, wide-eyed but smiling. "Man, that was close! When I dove I hit my head and it must have stunned me. For a minute there I couldn't feel anything. It was weird. It was like one of those times when you lay on your arm funny and it goes numb. Then I got a tingling sensation all over and the feeling came back." Mike's smile turned quizzical as he looked around, like something didn't add up.

"You all right?" Chuck asked once again.

"I'm fine, I'm fine," he replied defensively while forcing the smile back on his face. "Did anybody get a picture?"

"What? Are you nuts?" Chuck said incredulously.

"Colleen won't believe me when I describe the size of that boulder. You guys will have to back me up on it. You didn't happen to see any Lemurians, did you?"

"You're totally whacko!" I exclaimed and then started laughing uncontrollably. Mike started laughing, and then Chuck joined in, and we couldn't stop. There was a deep feeling of relief. We'd just dodged a speeding bullet, a major catastrophe. We gave each other 'I'm glad you're alive' hugs and then hastened our pace back down the mountain to Chuck's truck at the Bunny Flat trailhead.

When we got to Chuck's truck a park ranger was there waiting for us. He was a giant of a man. He must've been at least seven feet tall. He was aged, with pale skin, and had long silvery white hair tied up in a ponytail. His eyes were an intense steely blue. "I am the caretaker of this mountain. You are not supposed to leave anything on it," he said sternly.

Being the elder, more responsible one of our party, Chuck responded. "Not to worry sir, we were careful not to leave anything."

The ranger reached into his pocket, pulled out a camera, and then handed it to me. It was my Kodak Pocket Instamatic camera.

"I'm so sorry," I apologized, not realizing that it had been missing. "How'd you end up with it?" I'm thinking to myself, 'How could this guy have found my camera so rapidly and then beat us back to the truck. We'd come down from the summit rather quickly and I know I used it up there'.

"You're probably wondering how I could've found your camera so rapidly and beat you back down here," said the ranger. The hair stood up on the back of my neck. It was like he had read my mind. "I'll tell you, we watch this mountain like hawks. We help take care of Mother Nature. You better watch out for her too because she can take you out…" He started walking away, then looked back directly at Mike and finished with, "… for good." Then he walked off into the trees and vanished out of sight.

"Chuck, you see that? He was here, now he's gone. Now you see him, now you don't. And he was tall. I'm six feet one inch and he was looking way down at me."

"What're you hinting at Mark? You better get your steering wheel checked," he recommended. "I think it's come loose."

"Okay, wise guy, but how'd he get my camera and beat us back down here… and know what I was thinking?"

"I'm sure there's a logical explanation for it all. Did you hit your head on a rock when you dove? Or maybe your imagination is running wild because of what Sue said."

"Bingo! That's it. It's Sue's fault. I was just messin' with you," I said with a chuckle. I didn't want Chuck to think I was nuts. Lemurian or no Lemurian, I still had questions. Later on, when we were alone back at Chuck and Sue's house, I asked Mike about it. He said he wondered the same thing too, only he didn't dare open his mouth after hitting his head up there. He knew that if he started talking like that his brother would have him at a hospital in a heartbeat. Mike also brought up something I hadn't thought about — how did the ranger know it was my camera? *Spooky!* Our ranger incident was destined to remain a mystery.

Mike then made me promise not to tell his brother something else he was about to say. I promised. "Back on the mountain when I hit my head and lost my feeling, do you remember the odd look I had after I sat up?"

"Yes."

"This is hard to explain, but I felt short."

"You felt short?"

"Yeah, I felt short. I felt compacted like a little munchkin, like my head was sitting right on top of my boots. And on the ride home, it was odd. I kept feeling like I needed a booster seat to see out the window. I could see out, but I kept feeling like I needed to stretch my neck to do so, like an ostrich or a giraffe."

"Dude, why didn't you say something?" I questioned with concern. "This could be serious."

"Because I knew it'd get better."

"Has it?"

"Yep! I feel just as tall as when we began our trip," my buddy beamed confidently. "Remember, mums the word."

"Okay, but if you start having any more problems we're going to get you to a doctor."

The next day, even though Mike and I hadn't said a thing, Chuck urged Mike to see a doctor. He said that a possible head or neck injury and paralysis was nothing to fool with. Mike refused. He insisted that he was okay, that he felt great. This got me thinking about the dream I had back in Maricopa.

"Gee, I know what it feels like to be paralyzed," I said.

Chuck looked at me warily, "You messin' with me again?"

"No, but I remember vividly what it was like from a dream I had."

I'd never mentioned my dream to Chuck and Sue. So I recounted the crash, Mike's death, my internal decapitation and subsequent hospital stay. I told them what it felt like to be totally paralyzed from the neck down. How I couldn't do a thing for myself, not even breathe. How I had to be hooked up to a respirator. How with not being able to move anything, including my arms, I had to be tube-fed or spoon-fed. That bathing, getting dressed, and toileting all had to be done for me. That if I had an itch on my face I'd have to yell for a nurse or somebody to help, and with no lung power my yell wasn't much louder than a whisper. That if I wanted to read a book somebody had to flip pages for me. It was extremely frustrating! I'll tell you, it was as if I barely existed. It was not much fun, I told them.

"I'm glad that didn't happen to me," Mike said thankfully.

"Me too," I agreed. "That was one difficult road to navigate; that was one Mt. Everest to climb; that was one…"

"Okay, Mark," Chuck cut in, "we get the picture. You're talking like it was real."

"It sure felt that way. Who knows where that dream came from."

"You must have watched a good hospital drama on TV or at the movies," Sue said. "Sometimes something you've seen or had to deal with in real life will trigger some fascinating dreams."

"I'll tell you, it got more interesting than that. After months of being totally paralyzed, that hospital gave up on me and wanted to kick me out. I was being doomed to a convalescent hospital where I would have soon died. The head doctor at another hospital heard about my case because it's rare to have someone survive their skull coming off their spine. He salivated at the chance to have his team of doctors try and help me. He was confident they could, but no promises were made. I was transferred to his facility where they discovered a missed problem, swelling of the brain. I was getting a big head."

"I could have figured that out," Chuck said. "I heard how you whipped my brother Bill in racquetball the other day. And he's pretty good."

"Willy put up quite a fight," I grinned, "for an old man," Bill was older than Chuck. "Say, do any of you happen to know what the cure is for water on the brain?"

"No. What is it?" Sue asked unwarily.

"A tap on the head." My answer was met with groans. "Actually, that's not too far off from what happened next. Another surgery was required where the surgeon did put a tube inside my head. It goes down to my heart and drains fluid away from my brain, like a continuous tap. My thinking cleared and I improved. Hmm, maybe that's why my doctor was the 'head' doctor."

"Are you sure this didn't happen to you?" Chuck asked in jest. "You've come up with some very detailed visions and strange thoughts."

"Maybe that's because his tube is clogged," Mike joked.

"Funny, guys. It goes on," I said. "I remember once when the tube did malfunction. It came apart and I got some brain splitting headaches. I couldn't think. And don't say it, I know what you're thinking, so what's new."

"Now you're reading my mind. You sure you're not a Lemurian?" Chuck teased.

"Honey," Sue intervened, "let him finish. This is interesting."

"Thanks, Sue." I continued, "My doctor determined that my tube had come apart. He needed to operate and soon. I was admitted to a hospital right across the street from his office. Fearing that they wouldn't be able to revive me if they put me to sleep for the operation, they kept me awake. It was gnarly! I could smell the stench of burnt bone dust as the saw blade cut into my skull. I could hear the sound of blood being suctioned off. I remember how the anesthesiologist kept staring intently into my eyes."

"Your dream was that vivid?" Sue said.

"It was like I was in a movie theater watching myself on the big screen. It's weird. I usually don't remember my dreams, but this one, it's uncanny, it's like I have total recall. I can feel the feelings. Sense the emotions. Hear the lights and see the sounds. Oops, reverse that," I grinned. "I just need to get it down on paper. When we get back to San Diego I plan on writing a book about our trip. I'll include the dream in it somehow. It alone was like a lifetime, at least up until I broke my neck the second time. That's when my dream ended."

"Whoa there. Hold your horses. What do you mean a second time?" Chuck responded, then looking at Mike said, "Mike, maybe you should reconsider doing the rest of the trip. This could be some kind of forewarning, an omen."

Mike chuckled, "You may be right. I've already fallen off..." He stopped suddenly. Uh-oh, he forgot that he wasn't going to say anything about the falls. Mike looked over at me.

"Might as well tell them now. Curiosity kills cats."

Mike told Chuck and Sue about the falls and why they happened. They were genuinely concerned but agreed to not say anything to our moms. No sense getting them all shook up. Then I told them how I broke my neck the second time, about the fall at the restaurant. Afterwards, I went back to tell them about my partial recovery from the first crash: the wheelchair phase; the walker phase; and the walking with a cane phase, at which time I had limited mobility and overall numbness. It was a blockbuster dream.

The rest of our visit with Chuck and Sue included much more leisurely activities. One of them was the three of us guys inner-tubing down the Sacramento River. An ice chest loaded with refreshments was strapped to another inner tube and floated with us. It was very relaxing. Several hours later, ten miles downriver, Sue picked us up. She took one look at us and shook her head. We were like three slices of bacon that'd been sizzlin' in the sun. Our burnt skin made for some uncomfortable days. With shoulders ablaze, any more backpacking was out. However, we did get in two shorter hikes where we picnicked and fished. Sue joined us. She put us guys to shame catching the biggest fish, a thirteen-inch rainbow trout.

With our journey about to continue I still had fishing on my mind. But what was I hoping to catch?

Chapter Five

Luck and a Lady

I t had been a wonderful week at Chuck and Sue's, but now, after hearty hugs and good-byes, it was time to resume our trip. Unlike the west-bound trailblazers of yore, our adventure was taking us east. As we biked along, it got more strenuous. We were heading up into the mountains and through the Plumas National Forest. This forest has over a million acres and is loaded with different types of fir and pine trees. There were your typical Charlie Brown Christmas trees, the scragglier-looking Coast Douglas-Fir, and then there were the more spacious heavier-branched White Firs. Towering Ponderosa Pines with their long green needles and Jeffrey Pines with their stouter cones and reddish colored bark were also everywhere. We rode through the towns of Plumas, and then through Storrie at an elevation of 1,785 feet. By nightfall we'd climbed to 3,342 feet and reached Quincy, another town that was started during the Gold Rush.

Our mountainous travels continued the next day on through Cromberg and then up to Beckwourth at elevation 4,911. The town and pass were named for James Beckwourth, an adventurer, trapper and trailblazer who operated an inn and trading post there back in 1851. Next came Chilcoot and ten miles later, Hallelujah Junction. That name kinda makes you want to shout, hey? Hallelujah! We were putting on some miles.

The following day we crossed state lines and entered Nevada. Reno was the next big town we came upon. Silver mining had made this a booming place back in the 1850s. In 1931 they passed a liberal divorce law which brought many people to the area. Gambling brought even more. As we rolled into town, I found a silver dollar on the ground. Was this a sign? The words of another song came to my mind. 'Sign, sign, everywhere a sign … do this, don't do that,… can't you read the sign?' The words 'do this' grabbed my attention.

"Mike, I'm feeling awfully lucky today. How about you?"

"What you gettin' at?"

"How 'bout we try our luck in one of these casinos?"

"How 'bout we don't," Mike answered. "I work too hard for my money. I don't want to throw it away."

"Come on, give it a shot. We'll only play a little."

"That's what they all say. Next thing they know, they're broke."

"Oh, come on, just a little," I pressured. "You can keep me accountable."

"Okay, if you insist," Mike consented hesitantly. "I'll go, but I'm just gonna' watch. I'm not gambling with you."

"Gamble? Nah, it's a sure thing little buddy. Look, there's the Silver Dollar Casino down the street. It's begging us to get our butts down there. And remember, I found that silver dollar. It's fate."

We checked our bikes in at the desk. They were all too eager to have these two high-rollers from California come in to pitter away their money. The room was dimly lit, veiled in a hazy cloud of smoke. You could hear roulette wheels turning, one-arm bandits spitting out coins, and a caller shouting out keno numbers. It was an electric place, abuzz with energy. We found a blackjack table and I sat on the stool. Mike stood behind me. I put my silver dollar on the table and was dealt two aces down. I flipped them over, split them, and doubled my bet. I was then dealt two face cards. "Yes!" and the dealer busted. I had two winning hands right off the bat.

"All right!" I cried out, turning to give Mike a high-five. I was hot. I was feeling it. A half hour more at that table and I was up by over a hundred bucks. Yes, this was my lucky day. From there I took my winnings and headed over to the slot machines. "Which one, Mike?"

"What do you mean, which one?" he retorted.

"You know, which one is going to hit? You're my lucky charm!"

"I don't know. How about this one here in the corner? It looks lonely. Maybe it wants to make a friend."

"Okay, here goes. Come on, lover." I put a silver dollar in the slot and pulled the lever. The wheels turned and 'chomp', it ate my dollar. I put another dollar in the slot. I pulled the lever again, and 'chomp', it got eaten too. Then another and another disappeared into the belly of this ravenous machine.

"Mike, you sure this is the right one?"

"Maybe she's saying 'can't buy me luv'. I'd give it a couple more whacks," Mike chuckled.

I put in another silver dollar and 'chomp', it was gone. "Hungry little devil, aren't you!" I said to the machine. I pretended to walk away, to spread my affections elsewhere, then returned. "Okay, lover, this will be my last spin with you, unless…," I warned. This time I put in three silver dollars. I pulled the handle. The wheels turned as I impatiently waited. *'Cha-chink,'* cherry. *'Cha-chink.'* cherry. The excitement mounted. *'Cha-chink,'* cherry. "Yes!" I shouted out. "I won!!" Lights flashed and bells kept ringing loudly as silver dollar after silver dollar came spitting out of my lover. A pile grew. "Yes!" I'D HIT THE JACKPOT! I gave Mike another high five. The casino cashier came over to give me the rest of my winnings, seven-hundred and fifty big ones. I was on fire, on a winning streak. I put three more silver dollars in, pulled the handle, and 'chomp', they were gone. "Sorry," I apologized as I affectionately patted the machine goodbye. "It's time to move on."

"What's next?" Mike asked. "You've really got it goin'."

"Say, you don't think my lover's going to feel jilted, do you?"

"She'll get over it," he smiled. "Some other guy will come along and take her for a spin. How 'bout we try our luck at Keno?"

"Our luck? You haven't even touched your wallet."

We went over to the Keno area, sat down in their plush leather chairs, and proceeded to fill out some Keno sheets. I picked out five random numbers. Mike decided to give it a whirl too and picked five numbers of his own. We turned in our sheets, paid the cashier a buck and a quarter each, and sat down to wait. The caller announced the game was closed and then turned on the machine that juggled the numbered balls. One by one a ball was ejected and the number read aloud. Neither one of us had even one called number marked on our sheets. Bummer! Not even one! We each filled out another sheet, turned them in, paid the cashier, and waited for the numbers to be called out again. This time I didn't get any and Mike only got one. Big whoop!

"This is why I don't like to gamble," Mike said. "Let's go It's a waste of money. They wouldn't have built these huge casinos if people like us weren't losing."

"Oh, come on, just one more time. I'll even pay for your next sheet."

"You're crazy, but if you're paying, I'm playing. I'm done wasting any more of my money. We still have to buy a canoe once we get to Minnesota."

"Dude, how easy you forget. I'm way ahead. I'm rocking and rolling."

We filled out two more sheets and turned them in. After the numbers were called, Mike didn't have any and I had three, enough to at least get my money back. So I played again. This time I decided to be more strategic with my numbers, 7, 21, 19, 55, for my birthday, which was a lucky day for me, and then a 1, which sounds like won. Long story short, after the numbers had all been called, I had a winner! $625.00! That's s--i--x-hundred twenty-five buckaroos. *YES!* Five for five! Mike rolled his eyes. He could not believe my luck.

"Mike, I can't help it. When you're hot you're hot." I was exuberant! Hey, it's what I expected. I was born to be a winner!

"Whatcha wanna do now? You ready to leave?" Mike asked.

In the background, I heard the sound of a little metal ball dancing around on a roulette wheel. That was my clue. It wanted to join in on the party. "Let's give the wheel a spin," I said. When we got to the table, the attendant announced, "Place your bets". I opted to wager on red or black, it was nearly a fifty-fifty chance. I played at that table for the next half hour. When I picked red, it went black. When I picked black, it went red. For the life of me I could not pick the right color. I only won a couple times. I tried a larger ten-dollar bet on red and the ball landed on 'OO' green. Bad omen.

"Looks like your lucky streak is over," Mike warned. "Let's go."

"Maybe roulette isn't my game. Let's go back to the blackjack table where it all began." There was a new dealer. Over the next hour I dropped over a hundred dollars. I would bust or the dealer would hit blackjack. Things had definitely taken a turn for the worse.

"Come on, Mark, let's get going. I think you've lost it."

"Just a little while longer. I'm simply having a bad run of luck. It'll turn."

Mike grabbed me by the arm and pulled me off the stool. I told the dealer to watch my chips, that I'd be right back. Out of range of the dealer's hearing, Mike chided me.

"Hey, buddy, you're way ahead. Don't give it all back. Remember, 'You can keep me accountable.' Those were your exact words."

"Don't worry. I've got it under control. I know how addicting this can be. Just two more hands and I'll cash in, and we'll be on our way. I promise."

Sure enough, I had two more losing hands. Quitting on a losing note didn't feel good. That was, thanks to Mike's urging, until I cashed in my chips. Yeah!! I had amassed a whopping fourteen hundred dollars. We retrieved our bicycles and stepped outside into the 'WHOA', it was blinding bright out here. It took a minute for our eyes to adjust to the daylight.

"Dang, Mike! We could've gotten jumped right there," I said with alarm.

"No kidding, and you've got all that money."

"Shh, shh, not so loud. This street looks kinda seedy. Let's find a bank and I'll wire it home to my mom."

We found a bank and took care of business. That was a relief. The fresh air outside was now much more noticeable. It had been a nice — and profitable — stop. The rest of that day we pedaled through high desert country. The riding wasn't too taxing thanks to some easier grades. On our way we traveled past the Humboldt Sink, a dry lakebed now used as a nesting area for birds. By dusk we neared the town of Lovelock where we set up camp for the night.

Humboldt, Winnemucca, and Orovada were the following days' stops as we continued through Nevada. Thousands of pioneers had passed through here on their journey west. I could picture them in covered wagons being pulled by weary horses. I could imagine the sounds of horses snorting and hoofs clomping on dry ground as they kicked dirt and dust up into the air. It must have been a spine-jarring journey, definitely not like pedaling on the smooth paved roads Mike and I got to ride on. And what about a flat tire, I mean a broken wagon wheel, or running out of water? They didn't have the convenience of Triple-A© and roadside assistance. Death was an ever-present possibility. They had to be terribly hardy and have lots of heart.

This brings two fellows to mind. They were more of the evil heart variety. If I remember correctly, Butch Cassidy and the Sundance Kid robbed a bank in Winnemucca. Then, to 'celebrate their withdrawal', they sent a picture of themselves to the bank president. Today many others in this area also love to take your money, only legally, working at casinos. Most others work for mining and potato-processing companies.

At a rest stop, we talked. "Mike, I was thinking about the pioneers who traveled this way and their bone-rattling trip. And then I got to thinking about my dream and my broken neck."

"What about your dream and your broken neck?" Mike asked.

"I was a mess. My skull actually got lifted off my spine."

"You mean you almost lost your head?"

"Yeah, literally. They had to fuse my spine all back together. I'll tell ya, I looked like Frankenstein. I had a metal band going around my head with bolts screwed into my skull. That was attached by rods to a bodycast which went from my shoulders down to my waist. They put me on a thing called a Stryker frame where you're looking at the floor for two hours, and then they flip you over and you're looking at the ceiling for two hours, and then they flip you over and you're looking at the floor for two hours, and... Flip, flop. Flip, flop. Like a pancake. One time when I was being flipped by a nurse I slipped out mid-flip and my head hit the floor. The nurse freaked. Blood was oozing out from where the bolts were screwed into my skull. It was gnarly! A morbid Halloween party. Just talking about it gives me the chills."

"Then put on a jacket."

"Cute. Talking about it keeps it fresh until I get it all written down."

"Sounds like one bad nightmare," Mike said.

"It was. Then there was this guy in the bed next to me. He left the party early. He went code blue and died. This was not a fun place."

"Yeah, that doesn't sound fun," Mike concurred.

"It wasn't. I was totally paralyzed from the neck down, for what seemed like an eternity."

"That part must've really got to you because you mentioned it at my brother's house too."

"It did. I was so distraught. At times I wished I could jump out the window and end it all, but I couldn't even move to do that. My mind was trapped in a body that had gone AWOL. I tell you, I was a pathetic case. I was worse off than what we talked about before our trip, you know, at my mom's when we made that pact."

"You, kill yourself? No way, you're too positive for that. I'll bet this dream of yours came about because of that discussion, like Sue said," Mike reasoned.

"Maybe. Let's get goin'."

We camped that night near Orovada. Mike and I got to talking about how this town got its name. We decided that somebody must've been really drunk and didn't know if they were in Oregon or Nevada.

The next day, after a couple hours of riding, we did enter Oregon. We went through McDermitt, over the Blue Mountain Pass, through Burns Junction, and ended up in Rome. It had been another good day's ride in the high desert elevations. We didn't spend too much time in Oregon because we were just passing through its southeast corner. The following day we crossed a river and bicycled past an antelope reserve where we saw a herd of them grazing in the distance. Then we rode into Jordan Valley, named after Michael Jordan, a prospector from the nineteenth century. Lots of Spanish people lived in this area, making their livelihood from cattle ranching and sheep herding. From there we headed across state lines into Idaho, then down to the town of Marsing, and on to Lake Lowell.

Lake Lowell is a popular recreational site with quite a variety of wildlife. We didn't see any yellow-tailed marmots or long-tailed weasels or raccoons as advertised, but we did see plenty of cottontail rabbits hopping about. Canadian Geese, Western Grebes, and Mallards were also seen. A picture sign display helped us pick them out. We opted to camp at this beautiful lake hoping to get a good nights' sleep. I wanted to be well rested for the coming day when we'd get to visit with Chelsea, a classmate of mine from high school. There was a curious sort of anticipation building inside me. I found out that back in our school days she had a crush on me. I seemed to remember her looking good but those memories were rather vague. I didn't really know her that well. Two questions needed answers. What did Chelsea look like now, and did she still have a spark for me? Who knew what lay ahead?

At the crack of dawn I was the first one up. The sounds of nature were coming alive. Geese were honking. Ducks were quacking. Little feet could be heard as a squirrel scampered up a nearby tree. Excitement was in the air. I got a fire started and began heating up a pot of water for some hot chocolate and oatmeal. Mike was still sound asleep. 'Should I?' I thought. Then I remembered my promise from last time I jumped on him. Better not. Instead, I got a cup of cold water, went over to him, and slowly let it drip onto his head.

"Whoa! Whoa! What's goin' on?" Mike roused.

"Time to get up, little buddy. You get to go meet Chelsea today."

"Man, I was having the best dream."

"Don't tell me that you're going to start this dream thing too!"

"Dude, I was riding a killer wave. I was right in the curl, just about to get tubed, and then you woke me," Mike said, a bit irritated.

"You're probably lucky I woke you, 'cuz you may have been about to get creamed. Banzai!" And I pounced on him still in his sleeping bag.

"Hey, you promised," Mike protested.

"'Fraid not. That's only if you're asleep."

We washed up, got our things together, and feeling refreshed we took off for Boise, Idaho's state capital. When we got there I found a pay phone, deposited my dime, and dialed my friend's number.

"Hello," someone answered.

"Hi, this is Mark Manion. Can I please speak to Chelsea?"

"Mark, this is Chelsea! Where are you?" she asked.

"We're here."

"No way, you're here already?" Chelsea responded in disbelief.

"Yes, we're here. It was a struggle, what with unmarked trails, broken-down wagon wheels, and Indian raids. It's turned out to be quite an adventure."

"Get out, where are you really?" she asked again.

"We are here, really. How do we get to your house?" And with that Chelsea gave us directions.

We found her house easily enough. As we walked up towards her door, I asked Mike how I looked. He told me not to worry about it, that I looked fine. Then he reminded me that I had a girlfriend. I told him no big deal, that I just wanted to look nice, and rang the doorbell. Chelsea answered.

"Mark, it's so good to see you!" she greeted warmly.

I was momentarily dumbstruck, couldn't even speak. Chelsea had been good-looking if I remembered correctly, but today she looked absolutely awesome! I'm thinking cover girl material. Never had I seen her look so good. She had on a beautiful peach-colored dress, set off by a serpentine gold necklace and matching dangle earrings. Her hair was gorgeous. Her smile was from ear to ear. It looked like she had spent a lot of time preparing for this moment. It was eerily similar to a part of my dream, the part that led to marriage. I couldn't wait to tell Mike about this.

"Hi," I managed to get out. I gave her a hug and she seemed to melt into my arms. When I looked into her eyes, they seemed to say, 'I love you, I'm yours'. Somebody slap me. Something clicked in my heart. But then reality grabbed hold of me, 'Hey, what's going on here? You've still got a girlfriend back in San Diego.' I slammed on the brakes. "Chelsea, I'd like you to meet my best friend, my cousin Mike."

They shook hands, then Chelsea brought us in to meet her parents. We spent the next few hours talking about our journey and then rehashed old school memories. We were in a couple of the same classes but didn't hang out together. I probably should have had my eyes checked. Her parents were gracious enough to allow us to stay in their spare bedroom downstairs. We were going to get to sleep in beds, another nice change from roughing it outdoors. After Chelsea and her parents went to bed, Mike and I chatted for awhile.

"Mike, did you see her?" I asked incredulously.

Looking puzzled Mike responded, "What do you mean, did I see her?"

"Her dress, her smile, the way she looked at me. Remember that dream I had back in Maricopa where I told you I got married? She looked just like that!"

"If you remember, we met two girls at that swimming pool, like you dreamed, and I'm not dead and you're not paralyzed."

"But, if you'll remember," I reminded, "we thwarted that part by going to their party."

"You and your dream. I think you need blinders, like some racehorses wear to keep on track. Remember Shari."

"Shari who?"

"Shari your girlfriend, you idiot!"

"I know. I'm just messin' with you. But I'll tell you, before we left on this trip, a few things were starting to bug me. She's Jewish and I'm Christian. How's that going to work out with raising children? And some of our interests seem to be going in way different directions. I love her, but…"

"You are a butt. Sounds to me like you're trying to rationalize Chelsea into your life. I'm sure glad I know who my girl is. Life is less complicated that way. By the way, what is Chelsea's faith?"

"I don't know."

"Yeah, you are a butt. Let's get some sleep. Good night."

The smell of frying bacon wafted through the house. What a pleasant aroma to wake to. When Mike and I walked out into the dining room, Mrs. Meyers, Chelsea's mom, had a breakfast feast already prepared. Bacon, eggs, pancakes, sausage, fruit slices, and glasses of orange juice adorned the table. It was a meal fit for traveling royalty. Chelsea and her parents ate with us. They were a friendly bunch. They told us we could stay as long as we wanted. Mike told them that it was a dangerous invitation to make after cooking such a scrumptious meal, that meals like that could make us long-term residents. Mrs. Meyers smiled and thanked Mike for the compliment.

"It's a beautiful day in the neighborhood," I commented.

"That it is," Mrs. Meyers agreed.

After breakfast, Chelsea and her mom left to go run some errands. While they were gone, I made a telephone call to my girlfriend back home. Shari's mom answered.

"Hi Mrs. Lutz, is Shari there?"

"Yes, one sec. I'll get her." A few moments later Shari answered the phone.

"Mark, how are you doing? I've missed you."

"I've missed you too. We're doin' fine. We're in Boise now, resting up for a few days before we continue on to Minnesota. What have you been up to?" I asked.

"Scuba-diving!" she squealed. "I'm really loving it! My instructor says I'm doing very well. He's been teaching scuba for years. He's really good!"

We talked for a few more minutes. I told her that I'd been sending postcards from each city to document our trip. She said she'd already gotten some and was putting them in a shoebox for me. I thanked her and told her that I had to get going.

"I love you. Can't wait 'til you get back," Shari said.

"I love you too," I replied. For some reason our conversation seemed a little distant. But of course, what did I expect, I was calling long-distance and we'd been apart for about three weeks.

"Mike," I yelled out to the other room.

"What do you want?" he called back.

"Mike, it's so like in my dream."

"Not your dream again. What's goin' on now?"

"I just got done talking with Shari and I know it sounds nuts, but she's really enjoying scuba-diving with her instructor."

"So what's the big deal?"

"Well, if you remember in my dream when I was totally paralyzed from the neck down, fluid was building up in my head and the doctors didn't realize it. I was slowly becoming a vegetable. Shari really hung in there, but after months of this and it looking like there was no hope for me, that this was what I would be like for the rest of my life, like a vegetable, well, she... Have you ever wondered why someone in that state is called a vegetable?"

"Mark, finish your story."

"Well, have you?"

"No, why?"

"I don't know. But you'd think they'd be called a pork sausage or a triple chocolate sundae, something not that good for you. Vegetables are a healthy part of one's diet."

"All right already, you pork sausage, what happened?"

"She fell for this scuba guy."

"Bummer. How'd that make you feel?" Mike questioned.

"I'll tell you, it didn't feel great. It sucked, but it was totally expected. I mean, at our age, what would you have done? Would you have stuck with that, a vegetable, for the rest of your life? I doubt it. We weren't even married."

"Sounds to me like you're using this dream to further rationalize your relationship with Chelsea," Mike voiced out-loud.

"What? Are you a psychoanalyst now? Maybe I should lay down on a couch." Inside my head, and my heart, I knew what he was saying was true. "Hey, Mr. Analyst, analyze this. It's a little story I heard the other day. Two carrots were walking down the sidewalk when all of a sudden a car came careening off the street and struck one of them. The uninjured carrot got his buddy checked in to a hospital and then waited impatiently. After awhile the doctor came out. 'I've got good news for you and I've got bad news,' the doctor informed. 'What's that?' the carrot buddy wanted to know. 'The good news is your buddy is going to live. The bad news, it looks like he's going to be a vegetable for the rest of his life.'"

Mike chuckled. "If you got hit by a car you'd be a squash."

"I hope the ladies 'turnip' soon. It's getting kinda deep around here."

When Chelsea got back we spent the day touring her city. She told us that Boise is nicknamed the 'City of Trees', that it is a French word meaning 'wooded'. She said that French/Canadian fur-trappers had exclaimed "Les Bois!" when they crossed the mountains and looked down into the valley. Part of Chelsea's tour was a visit to the capital building, an impressive structure made out of native sandstone and marble. It was a very relaxing day, for our bicycles too.

The next few days Chelsea took us around the outer-lying areas of Boise. There were majestic forests, pristine lakes, peaceful meadows, and meandering rivers. There were towering mountains. Lots of them! There was also Chelsea. She drove us a few hours to Sun Valley, Idaho, a place where I'd always wanted to ski. How cool was that seeing as downhill skiing was my favorite sport? It turned out that Chelsea loved it too. Mike had never skied before, but even so, we'd already talked about moving to Mammoth Mountain for the upcoming winter. It's a big ski resort in central California.

When we reached Sun Valley we took a lift up the mountain. I envisioned myself, and a certain someone, skiing down these soon to be snow-covered slopes. They sure were pretty. Chelsea could only add to their beauty. Maybe I was jumping the gun, but it was a fun thought. We all enjoyed the views, then descended back down to the lodge for something to eat.

"How would the two of you like to get in some tennis?" Chelsea asked after lunch.

"You're talking one of my favorite games," I answered enthusiastically. "I played on our high school tennis team."

"I remember that. I was so proud of how well you did," Chelsea beamed.

"You were?"

"Yes, I was. I was your biggest unknown fan."

"Wow, I never knew." More kindling was being added to a flickering flame growing inside me. With that we went to the pro shop, borrowed some racquets, and had a rousing game of tennis. One of Chelsea's girlfriends showed up and we played mixed doubles for the rest of the afternoon. The day well spent, we headed back to Boise. This was going to be our last night there before resuming our trip. When we arrived at Chelsea's home, Mike went inside and I stayed out on the porch with Chelsea.

"I had a very good time here with you," I said.

"So did I."

"So you had a good time with you too?" I kidded.

"No, with you. You know what I mean."

"I know."

"Will I ever get to see you again?" Chelsea asked.

"I hope so. You know, I love to ski, and I've always wanted to ski at Sun Valley. This winter I'd love to come back and do some skiing with somebody I know here."

"I'd like that... a lot!"

"I'd like that too." With that I gave her a hug and a kiss on the cheek, and we went inside to join Mike.

Chapter Six

Pedal Mettle

The next day Mike and I said our good-byes and resumed our journey. From Boise we pedaled southeast to a town called Mountain Home. It used to be a stagecoach stop but has since become the home of an Air Force base. We got a VIP tour of the base and learned that it opened during World War II and was used for bomber training. After our tour we got a lot of coercion by a recruiter to enlist. We politely said no thanks to his offer and continued on our way. From there we pedaled east and uphill until we reached Hill City. There we camped for the night.

The following day we headed through Fairfield and eventually reached the turn-off to Sun Valley where we'd just visited. It drove home the point about how much faster travel is by car. It also brought up thoughts of Chelsea and a little dilemma I was struggling with — what to do with these new-found feelings for her. At the junction to Sun Valley we considered a short detour the other way to the Shoshone Indian Ice Caves which I'd read about. The caves have an interior temperature of 18-28 degrees. That's quite intriguing when you realize that only a few feet above at the surface it could be over 100 degrees. It gave me an idea, a mental picture of what I should do with Chelsea. Simply put my hots for her on ice.

We passed on the caves and continued our ride. We rode through Picabo and came to the Craters of the Moon National Monument and Preserve, an 1,100 square-mile area where Basaltic volcanic activity occurred 2,000 years ago. There were lava beds and lots of dark porous rock as far as the eye could see. This landscape enhanced the mental picture of my ordeal. Let me spell it out for you. Hots. On ice. Now a meltdown. Do you get it? I'll tell you, when you ride a bicycle for so many hours you have a lot of time to think, perhaps in this case, too much. It had been a grueling hot day of riding. Maybe I was suffering from heat exhaustion. Our day ended at Arco.

Mike and I found out that back in 1951, Arco was the first area to get nuclear-powered energy. It's quite amazing how far we've come along, from pre-historic lava flows to covered wagons to nuclear-powered energy. Who knows, perhaps someday we'll all have wireless communicators like on Star Trek where we'll be able to talk to one another from almost anywhere. Then we wouldn't need to carry a pocketful of change for pay phones. Wouldn't that be nice — no more dropped calls after an operator interrupts your call, "to continue deposit another 25 cents" and you can't scrounge up the extra change.

As Mike rolled up his sleeping bag the next morning I commented, "Mike, you must have had a really good night's sleep."

"Why's that?" he responded suspiciously.

"You just seem to be radiating with energy today."

"Funny guy, you look like you're all aglow too."

We got out our trusty map to determine where we wanted to go. With all this new-found nuclearized energy, knowing it would add a couple hours to our ride, we decided to visit Idaho Falls. There's something about seeing waterfalls that sparked our interest. The town of Idaho Falls sprang up when rich discoveries of gold and silver were found nearby. It was also one of the few places where one could ford the upper Snake River. I wondered if anybody ever tried to chevy it. Sorry. Again, too much time to think. Somebody better grab the pen out of my hand before I go hog wild. When we did arrive at the falls, it was definitely worth the ride. The waterfall, which is on the Snake River, is not very high but it is over a thousand feet wide and very turbulent. It gave us one of those Kodak© picture moments. It got us thinking about our upcoming canoe trip.

"Hey, Mark, how'd you like to get sucked over those falls?" Mike queried.

"It wouldn't be pretty. We'll have to watch for that once we get to Ely and start canoeing."

"Yeah, and not just on rivers, lakes too. I remember reading that they can also have a current that'll draw you into harm's way. Going over a waterfall or getting pulled into some violent rapids could be disastrous."

"That's why we brought binoculars," I said smugly, like we'd thought of everything. "We can scope it out and prevent that from happening. We came prepared."

"Yes, we did," Mike agreed.

Mike and I had diligently prepared for this whole trip. We were both extremely confident, positive, can-do-anything type thinkers. The canoeing part was going to be a snap. Besides, look how well we'd fared up to now. We'd only been knocked off our bicycles once. Of course, Mike did have that one little fall coming down from King's Canyon, and then there was that incident climbing at Mt. Shasta, but who's counting, we lived through all that. We'd even managed not to get sucked under passing semis hauling those monster double-trailers behind. I'll admit, that had scared me at times, especially when they got so close we could have reached out and touched their tires. The point is, we are survivors. Canoeing was probably going to be the easiest part of our trip. Rather than pedal, we'd just get to go with the flow. It wasn't a concern of ours that neither one of us had ever canoed before. Or should it have been?

We camped by the falls that night. At first it was hard to go to sleep with that constant roar in the background, but eventually it had a numbing effect and we slept almost as if in a coma. The next couple days we pedaled north along the Continental Divide. We went up and over the Monida Pass, from Idaho into Montana, then down to the valley, the valley so low. Makes you want to start singing, hey? Kinda reminds me of a tune I learned in elementary school. Dillon, Montana is in that valley and is surrounded by other rich fertile valleys. We were told they have some of the best cattle-raising and hay growing in the state.

"Hey, Mike," I asked as we rode, "do you ever wonder how they come up with the names of some of these towns?"

"Not really," he answered.

"Take this next town for example, Twin Bridges, why do you think they call it Twin Bridges?" I pondered aloud.

"Dude, you on drugs? That's so obvious."

"Not on drugs, just vitamins, same as you. That reminds me of another part of the dream I had back in Maricopa. I'll tell you about it after we solve this problem."

"What problem?!"

"The name of the town problem."

"Dude, it's so obvious. They named the town after two bridges they'd built that look alike."

"No, no. Mike, you have to think outside the box. Think about it — Lewis and Clark. Pioneers of old. Blazing new trails."

"So?"

"So, think about it," I went on. "In those times dentists weren't that available, so people could have had some really bad teeth problems. Problems that could be similar. Lewis and Clark, bridgework, get it?"

"Mark, who let you out of the box? Okay, now let's hear about your dream. I know you won't let it rest until you tell me about it."

"When we got hit by that drunk driver our belongings got scattered all over the highway, including our vitamins. Seeing pills everywhere, the highway patrol officer who arrived must've thought we were two druggies and got what we had comin' to us. It led to a rather sloppy investigation. The driver of the car wasn't even tested for alcohol or other drugs. In fact, that car had been pulled over just an hour before they hit us. And get this, that officer simply made them pour their beer out on the side of the road and let them go. I was furious! I wanted to wake up and shake some sense into that guy. It was horrible! Dude, you shouldn't have died and I shouldn't have been in a wheelchair." I was visibly upset again by this part of my dream.

"Chill, dreamer. Sounds like a bum deal but let's get back to reality." Mike said cracking a smile, amused over my animation at how seriously I was taking it. He continued, "But I'm not dead and you're not in a wheelchair. How cool is that?"

"Way cool," I replied. "And you know what?"

"What?"

"You and me, we're living our dream."

"That we are," Mike agreed with a sense of satisfaction.

Next we toured the Lewis and Clark caverns, beautiful multi-colored limestone caves with some exquisite formations. They truly were a creative work of God. We continued on from there to Three Forks, Montana. I didn't have the heart to tell Mike what I was thinking about that name. I didn't want to exasperate him any further. It seemed rather funny to me though. Three Forks I imagined as a very ritzy place that got its name from a table setting at a swanky restaurant. You know, where you have three forks; one for the appetizer, one for the salad, and one for the main meal. Three Forks actually got its name because of three nearby rivers that joined together to form the Missouri River.

Miles later came Bozeman, a touted recreational area with excellent trout fishing. All our fishing gear and backpacking equipment had been shipped ahead to Minnesota from Chuck's home so we didn't do any fishing there. As we pedaled, we climbed over the Bozeman Pass and headed down to Livingston. Livingston is at the head of Paradise Valley and is surrounded by the Gallatin National Forest. It lies between two ranges of the Rocky Mountains. When we reached Livingston we decided to take another little detour from our eastward-bound route and headed south to Yellowstone National Park. It would be unimaginable and just plain rude to not visit Yogi and his pal Boo-Boo while we were in the area. After all, how many times had the two of them visited us at home on Saturday mornings.

Our little side trip into Yellowstone took us three days. We traveled through densely wooded areas. It was another visual wonderland. There were seething hot springs, bubbling mud pots, and water spewing geysers, all relieving the earth's intense pressure. Again this reminded me of another part of my dream. It had to do with the two piece tube they put inside my head called a shunt. Years after its installation the pieces somehow got disconnected. Oh my goodness! Fluid amassed and pressure built. My head felt like it was going to explode, just like one of these geysers. I was sure somebody would find me dead with my brains splattered on the surrounding walls. An emergency operation fixed the problem and one month later I was thinking clearly again. Amazing! I decided not to bother Mike with this particular story, though. Didn't want to wear him out with too much dream talk. But it was all still so fresh in my mind, how I learned to walk again, my dating experiences, the… Boy, that dream really did have a whole life of its own.

We rode through Corwin Springs and Mammoth Hot Springs. As we continued riding we encountered some humungous mountains. We pedaled up and over the Colter Pass, and then the Beartooth Pass which was about two miles high. We're talking major cardiovascular exercise. Our tortured lungs and legs were begging for a reprieve. Coming down from Beartooth, we passed through Red Lodge, a busy resort area. In 1896 it was known for its riotous living and its twenty saloons. I could imagine saloon girls in skimpy outfits, cowboys with boots and stirrups, holsters packing six-shooters, the smell of rawhide, the ol' west. "Hey bartender, gimme a beer, and one for the lady," he'd shout as he slapped his gold piece on the bar. Mike and I didn't try that.

We crossed the Yellowstone River in route to Billings, Montana. Lewis and Clark traveled through here on their expedition. There's a natural feature called The Rimrocks which runs the length of the city and farther. The rocky formation is about four-hundred feet tall and overlooks the city and the Yellowstone Valley. A trail, the Chief Black Otter Trail, runs along its edge offering some panoramic views. Mike and I decided to skip the views and just ride through the valley as we headed east. We also were getting a little antsy to reach Ely and spend some time with our grandparents at their lake.

We rode through Hardin and into Crow Agency which is the capital city of the Crow Indians. The Little Big Horn Battlefield is nearby. We saw it and the monument commemorating this historic event. It's where Custer took his last stand. Again, it was a truly nostalgic experience, like being transported back in time. One could hear battle cries, muskets firing, and the sound of arrows swishing through the air.

Next in route came Busby, then Lame Deer.

"Hey, Mike, why do you think they call it Lame Deer?" I asked. "Just kidding." It didn't really matter anyway, Mike wasn't listening to me. He was probably deep in thought thinking of his girl back home. The riding was fairly easy up and down rolling rangeland. We kept clicking off towns, mile after mile, as we traveled. Broadus, Boyes, Hammond, and Alzada all came and went. The last town, Alzada, is known for a famous gun battle featuring cattle rustlers and the local authorities. The rustlers were known as the Exelby Gang. Then came Belle Fourche which means "Beautiful Fork." It too wasn't named for fine dining, but because it became a thriving center after the Gold Rush of 1876. It's near the center of the United States. We saw more ranches and farms as we rode through this area.

It didn't take much imagination to figure out the name for our next stop, Spearfish. Indians used to spear fish in the creek supplying food for the mining camps in the surrounding hills. The hills are called the Black Hills. It's not because the hills are black, they just look dark because of the tremendous amount of pine trees growing on them. The Lakota Sioux Indians revered the hills and would seek guidance from their ancestors there. We pulled off the road near the Sturgis turnoff to study our maps. Off to the left was Bear Butte State Park.

"Hey, Mike, keep your eyes looking straight forward," I cautioned.

"Why's that?" Mike questioned.

"I don't think Colleen would approve."

"Approve of what?"

"You looking at bare butts."

"You know, I really miss Colleen."

"Yeah, I miss Shari too."

On checking our map, Rapid City, South Dakota, was the next major town we'd come to. From there, a right turn and some backtracking would take us to Mount Rushmore. It looked like more uphill mountain riding was involved.

"What do you think Mike? Should we visit the presidents?"

"I don't know. My legs are getting a little weary. What do you think?"

I reached into my pocket and pulled out some change. "Mike give me a dollar bill."

"What do you want that for?"

"Just give me one and I'll show you."

Mike handed me a dollar bill. I set it on the ground and then from the change I pulled out of my pocket I put a penny and a nickel to the left of Washington's face and a dime to the right. Then I laid down next to them.

"Okay, Mike, take a picture."

"What?"

"You know, take a picture. It'll be my head with the four president's heads; Lincoln's head on the penny, Jefferson's on the nickel, Washington's on the dollar, and Roosevelt's on the dime. That's as close as we're going to get to those granite heads on this trip. Go ahead, take a picture and I'll get one of you." Looking skyward while posing I saw some ominous looking clouds rolling in. "Hurry up, it looks like we're going to be in for some rain."

Mike laughed while posing for his picture.

"What's so funny?" I asked.

"When we looked at our map I saw a town called Rockerville on the way to Mount Rushmore. I could visualize a bunch of old geezers in rocking chairs rocking away on their front porches. Dude, that could be us someday."

The exuberance we had at the start of our trip had waned. We'd seen lots of beautiful country. I think our last trek through the mountains had taken a toll on us, both mentally and physically. Side trips had now lost their appeal. For example, we were coming up to the town of Wall and just south of there was the Badlands National Park, another pictorial buffet of weathered and eroded land featuring cliffs, ravines, and spired ridges. Wall is famous for the Wall drug store opened during the Depression. And drugstores are a great place to buy postcards. So rather than pedal the extra distance to see the Badlands, we bought postcards of them. Our legs welcomed the relief. For now Mike and I were on a mission, to get to our grandparents' house. You know, over the river and through the woods to Grandmother's house we go.

We spent the next few days riding through South Dakota. Minnesota was right next door. We rode through Philip and Midland on our way to Pierre, South Dakota's capital. The ride brought us through more cattle ranches and farmland. As we rode, Miller, Wolsey, Huron, Des Smet, Arlington, and Brookings all became towns in our rear-view mirrors, so to speak. Then, *tada!* We crossed into Minnesota, our destination state.

Our first night was spent camping at Lake Benton near the state border. The next day we started riding towards Le Center. We opted to make it a two-day ride. My mom was born and raised in this area and still had relatives living there. My father grew up in Minneapolis. City boy meets country girl, and we're talking a very big city with lots of people and tall buildings in stark contrast to a very small rural farming town surrounded by lots of corn and wheat fields.

"Hey, Mike, you wanna hear a joke I heard? Riding past all these fields brought one to mind."

"Okay, let's have it," Mike replied.

"There were these two blonde ladies driving down the road in their convertible. There were wheat fields on both sides of them. One of the blondes commented, 'Will you look at that, that's what gives us blondes a bad rap.' Off in the middle of the wheat field was another blonde in a rowboat rowing away. In response to her friend's comment the other blonde responded, 'Yeah, I know what you mean. If I knew how to swim I'd swim out there and knock some sense into her.'"

We rode through Florence, Tracy, Springfield, and then when we arrived at New Ulm we rented a room for the night. I wanted to make a good impression on my relatives the next day. A good night's sleep and a shower couldn't hurt. Founded by a German immigrant and named for the German city called Ulm, New Ulm is a big center for brewing. It's also the polka capital of the nation. That reminded me of my short-lived stint on the accordion. When I was younger I'd taken lessons for about six months, but then Mom got pregnant with my little sister. My playing drove her up the wall. Goodbye accordion! There went my polka accompanying musical career.

The following day we pedaled through a number of small farming towns, Nicollet, St. Peter, and Cleveland, before reaching Le Center. We showed up at my Uncle Al and Aunt Dorothy's house in town. Uncle Al had a grading company he started after salvaging a bulldozer from the bottom of a lake. One company's loss became his sunken treasure. A couple of snowmobiles sat outside awaiting the upcoming winter. After being greeted warmly we spent the night there and the next day Uncle Al brought us out to my Grandpa Pete's farm. Grandpa had retired and didn't actually run the farm any longer, but he still lived there. My Uncle Tom now ran the show. He raised acre upon acre of wheat, feed-corn, flax, and peas. He was constantly rotating crops to maintain a balance of nutrients in the soil.

We drove down a long dirt and gravel driveway to get to Grandpa Pete's farmhouse. A hand-pumped well for water was in the side yard next to it. We walked up the steep wooden stairs and entered his very old country home. There was an antique floor-standing radio along one wall. Shelves with mason jars full of homemade jams and jellies and pickles and such lined the other walls. Bottles of my grandpa's favorite drink, Welch's grape juice, sat there among them. A vine wrapped around the room up by the ceiling. Off to the right was Grandpa's bedroom. It had an antique four-poster bed. Downstairs in the basement he still had an old Maytag© hand wringer-washer and a metal washtub. There was a musty smell in the air down there. This was a place stuck in time. Decades had passed without change. This was very country.

After checking out my grandpa's place we went next-door to my great Uncle Leo's farm. We drove. Next-door is different out in the country than it is in the city; it could mean a mile or more. Uncle Leo's two sisters, Aunt Agatha and Aunt Magdeline, lived with him. One was a retired schoolteacher, the other had been their stay-at-home cook and house cleaner. That was in the past. They'd since become world class pack rats, but very sweet ones. Their house was crammed wall to wall with stacked boxes of collected things hoarded over the years. I wouldn't be surprised if they'd saved every school paper they'd ever done and every knick-knack they'd ever received. There were narrow paths to walk through to get from one room to another. It was a maze. On their demise somebody was going to get a major migraine sorting through all this stuff.

Outside was their amazingly wonderful vegetable garden. These elderly ladies knew gardening. They treated us to a piece of homemade gooseberry pie made with berries fresh from their garden. It was to die for!

After that we then went to Uncle Tom and Aunt Lois' house for supper. They too owned a big farm. And they had a big family — thirteen children in all! Having two brothers and four sisters Mike thought he had a large family. This one astonished him. With a twinkle in his eye and a mischievous grin on his face, my uncle reminded him that winters there can be very long and very cold. He also reminded him that it takes a lot of work to run a farm. Mike got the picture. It wasn't quite like San Diego where you might find him surfing in the middle of winter.

The whole family showed up to greet us. There were aunts and uncles and cousins and second cousins and… People just seemed to come out of the woodwork. It was a large gathering, and everyone was so hospitable. We were served chicken as the main dish. It was fresh chicken too. How fresh was it? Let's just say that the birds had been running around in the yard clucking that morning. After supper — lathered in bug repellant — we all went out front to relax and play a game of softball. The front yard was big. It was so big that it actually had a playing field with a baseball diamond on it. It was a field of dreams and it got a lot of use. Big farm, big family, big meal, big yard, big game, and then finally came the big hugs and lots of encouragement for the rest of our trip. They made Mike and me feel like two heralded warriors about ready to head back into battle.

It's an interesting word, battle. Battles usually have victors and losers. Oftentimes casualties occur. On our trip across the country Mike and I had seen numerous cemeteries filled with fallen warriors. Would we be seeing any more? We would. The next short leg of our trip was to my Uncle Clair's house. He lived by one.

Chapter Seven

Boo Shoo and the Grim Reaper

Uncle Clair, one of my favorite uncles, lives in Minneapolis, Minnesota, one of the twin cities. Clair is my mom's brother. He's single, a schoolteacher/counselor, and a very witty guy. Uncle Clair is also a very fastidious person. Everything meticulously had its place. When you opened a desk drawer there was no scrounging around looking for anything. Pencils had their little box, paper clips had their little container, and notepads had their spot in the drawer. It was a very structured environment, my uncle's home. During summer breaks from school my uncle always went on trips to different parts of the world. Each trip was methodically researched so that he knew exactly where he was going, what he was going to see, and who lived in that particular area. We were hoping to spend the night at his house before heading north.

"Boo-shoo," Clair greeted us at the door.

"Boo shoo," I mimicked. "What are you doing, Uncle Clair? Trying to scare us off? We just got here."

Clair chuckled. "Hello. Boo-shoo means hello in Ojibwa. It's spelled with a 'z', b-o-o-z-h-o-o, but it sounds like an 's'."

"Boo-shoo," Mike said smiling as I introduced him to my uncle.

Clair knew about our final destination, Ely. So, being the thoughtful teacher that he was, he'd already researched that area for us. We got a history lesson. The Ely area was first inhabited by the Sioux Indians. That area and the area north of it, which later became known as the BWCA (Boundary Waters Canoe Area) had plentiful fishing, fur-trapping, and a bounty of wild blueberries. The story goes that the Ojibwa, who lived in the east, got a heavenly vision and followed a burning candle in the sky. The candle finally settled on the east coast of Lake Superior. From there warring parties fought over the lakes in that region. It was a hundred-year fight whereupon the Ojibwa eventually pushed the Sioux into the Plains.

In the 1700's French trappers and voyagers entered the area. In the mid 1800's when the Gold Rush began, explorers and prospectors searched for gold there only to find huge stores of iron ore. This led to huge open pit mines which eventually turned into deep mines. These mines needed to be supported by timbers and thus a logging industry was created.

Uncle Clair went on. Mike and I were getting our master's degree in the history of Ely. Immigrants, especially from the Scandinavian countries, looking for a better life funneled down into Ely. Many of them found themselves working in the mines. This was a very hard life. The miners had to work underground in a dark, dingy atmosphere wearing miner's caps with candles on them to illuminate the area where they worked. I couldn't imagine how tough that must've been. Clair told us there were 152 deaths in cave-ins and mudslides in the mines between 1889 and when the mines finally closed in 1967. He said that when there was a cave-in, a whistle blew for ten minutes to let people know what was happening. It was known as the "screamer." Not exactly what the immigrants had hoped for coming into this country. That is why many of these disillusioned immigrants committed suicide. In fact, for every death in the mines there were five deaths by suicide.

After our lesson and some small talk Uncle Clair took us out for dinner to his favorite restaurant, Jax. When we returned to his house Mike and I wanted to go for a walk and stretch out our legs. Clair lived right across the street from a fenced-in cemetery. We were going to walk around it. It was dusk.

"Hey, Mike, you wanna hear another joke?" I asked while we walked.

"What are you, a joke book? Where do you come up with all these jokes?"

"I don't know. I just hear them. Half of them I don't even remember, but the cemetery reminded me of one."

"Okay, let's have it," Mike said.

"On the outskirts of a small town," I started, "there was a big, old pecan tree just inside the cemetery fence. One day, two boys filled up a bucketful of nuts and sat down behind a gravestone by the tree, out of sight, and began dividing the nuts. 'One for you, one for me. One for you, one for me,' said one boy. In the process of counting the nuts, several dropped out of their hands and rolled down towards the fence. Outside of the fence, another boy came riding down the road on his bicycle. As he passed by, he thought he heard voices from inside the cemetery. He slowed down to investigate. Sure enough, he heard, 'One for you, one for me. One for you, one for me.' He just knew what it was. He jumped back on his bike and rode off. Just around the bend he met an old man with a cane, hobbling along. 'Come here, quick,' said the boy, 'you won't believe what I heard! Satan and the Lord are down at the cemetery dividing up the souls.' The man said, 'Beat it kid, can't you see it's hard for me to walk?' When the boy insisted though, the man hobbled with him to the cemetery. Standing by the fence they heard, 'One for you, one for me. One for you, one for me...' The old man whispered, 'Boy, you've been telling the truth. Let's see if we can see the Lord.' Shaking with fear, they peered through the bars of the wrought iron fence, yet were still unable to see anything. The old man and the boy gripped the iron bars of the fence tighter and tighter as they tried to get a glimpse of the Lord. Suddenly they heard, 'One for you, one for me. That's all. Now let's go get those nuts by the fence and we'll be done.' They say the old man made it back to town a full five minutes ahead of the boy on the bike."

Mike laughed, "That's a good one."

I agreed.

Some clouds had rolled in overhead making it unusually dark. A streetlight came on casting spooky shadows around us. A chilly breeze began to blow. Fallen leaves swirled about on the sidewalk. And then came the heart attack.

"Boys," boomed a deep throaty voice from behind us. "What are you up to?"

Mike and I nearly jumped out of our shoes as we quickly turned around. There he stood, the Grim Reaper. He was a man at least seven feet tall, wearing a stovepipe hat and a long black trench coat. His face was pale white. He had carbon black eyelashes and dark steely eyes that could bore a hole right through you. This guy was Frankenstein plus.

"We're just on a walk," I stammered. Mike shook his head in agreement but looked like he was ready to bolt. The wind gusted.

"I'm the caretaker of this here cemetery. I watch over the bodies of the dead resting here. I wouldn't want anything to happen to them. Understand?" the Grim Reaper emphasized.

"You don't have to worry about us, we're on our way home," Mike said adamantly.

"Something tells me I'm going to see one of you boys soon," the Grim Reaper chortled from his gut. A streak of lightning flashed above immediately followed by a deafening crack of thunder. Raindrops began to fall.

A little shaken by this eerie encounter, we watched as the caretaker walked down the street and disappeared out of sight.

As we hurried home Mike asked, "What do you think he meant when he said that he'd see one of us soon?"

"I don't know, I think he's just trying to scare us, to make sure we don't mess with his cemetery," I answered.

"That guy gives me the creeps," Mike stated.

"Me too," I agreed. "He's worse than that old kook at Mt. Shasta."

When we got home we told Uncle Clair about the Grim Reaper. Clair smiled and then told us that this fellow likes to tease kids. Teasing or not, Mike and I were in total agreement, this guy had some kind of mental derangement.

The bicycling portion of our trip was coming to an end. Mike and I only had about three-hundred miles to go to reach Ely. We decided to make it a four-day ride. After a nice breakfast at Uncle Clair's we gave him hugs and began pedaling north. We went through Rush City, and then Pine City, which used to be an Indian village. Then came Hinckley. Uncle Clair had informed us that Hinckley had been burned down in 1894 by a forest fire. It was one of the worst on record, burning over four-hundred square miles of forested land. Next up was Sandstone which is situated along the Kettle River. We learned that it had great rapids for kayaking and canoeing. This really whet our appetites for our upcoming canoeing adventure.

Deluth was the next big city that we came to. It was located in a hilly area bordering Lake Superior. We rode along the lakeshore and crossed the railroad tracks at Two Harbors. Interestingly enough, we found out that the tracks went all the way to Ely. Prior to the mines closing, iron ore had been brought here by rail from Ely and then shipped out from there. The area had lakes, parks, waterfalls, and an old lighthouse that we got to tour. Beaver Bay and Silver Bay were next, more lakes, more parks, and another lighthouse. When we hit Elgin City we left the lake and headed northwest towards Ely.

At last! We reached the turnoff, a dirt road that led to our final destination. We pedaled down that road through the woods and then, Shazam! there it was, our grandparents' 'cabin'. When Grandpa and Grandma started building their home it was supposed to be a cabin, but eventually it turned into a beautiful two-story house with opulent lake views. It was built on the woodsy point of Eagle's Nest Lake. In the middle of this pristine lake is a wooded island. It's an absolutely gorgeous spot, a Garden of Eden! There was Grandpa off to the right stacking cut logs in his woodshed for the upcoming winter.

"Grandpa!" Mike exclaimed.

"Well, look what the north wind blew in," Grandpa responded with a smile.

"Grandpa," I too said. Mike and I parked our bicycles and went to greet him. He gave us hearty handshakes. Grandpa was a retired railroad man. He was wearing his gray and black suspendered overalls and a matching railroad cap.

"Why don't you two run up to see your grandmother. She'll be so excited. We've been expecting you. I think she has something yummy already prepared." Mike and I scurried up the stairs and knocked on the screened porch door.

"Who is it?" Grandma called out.

"Who do you think it is, Grandma?" Mike replied.

"Boys, boys, come on in. I'm so glad you're here." Our white-haired Grandma came out of the kitchen wearing an apron and gave us each a big hug. There was a wonderful smell wafting into the dining room area where we met. "You two sit here at the table. I baked you some chocolate chip cookies and I'll bring you each a glass of milk to go with them." A couple of moments later Grandpa came plodding up the stairs. He left his boots at the door, changed into his slippers, and then sat down to enjoy the refreshments with us.

"I see that the flagpole is still standing," I commented.

"Oh, my lord!" Grandma exclaimed, "That day still brings shivers up my spine!" Grandpa smiled.

"Mike, did I ever tell you about one of the most terrifying experiences of my life?" I asked.

"No, what's that?" he responded.

Grandma put her hands over her ears. "I don't know that I could stand to live this all over again," she said, unamused.

"Don't worry, Grandma, what's done is done." And I proceeded to tell Mike the story about the flagpole.

Years ago, when I was still in junior high school, my whole family had come here to visit for a few days. Grandpa had just installed a new flagpole. The pulley at the very top was jammed and not working. My father, God rest his soul, volunteered me to fix it. Grandpa got out a ladder and set it up next to the flagpole but it only went half the height of the pole. They wanted me to climb all the way up and above the ladder to reach the pulley. I protested.

"How is that spindly top of the flagpole going to support me," I asked.

"Don't worry. You've got good balance. You can do it," they responded.

Easy for them to say — they weren't doing the climbing. They seemed to have no doubt though that I could do it. Not to be one that went against my father's wishes, I looked up and started climbing. When I neared the top of the ladder I still had a ways to go. My heart began pounding loudly. I was sure Mom and Grandma could hear it. Looking out the plate-glass window, they watched from the house and were visibly shaken. I thought I heard the hammering of somebody already building my coffin. It was a long way to the ground and an early death. I was too young to die.

What happened next is simply a blur in my memory. I think my brain must have shut down in fear. Somehow I managed to reach the top, get the pulley fixed, and get back down that ladder in one piece. It is something I swore I'd never do again. To commemorate the occasion my whole family and Grandpa and Grandma had a flag-raising ceremony. We all pledged allegiance to the flag and to the United States of America for which it stands.

Mike then started telling about his stay here last summer. He'd spent several weeks at The Dove, which is what our grandparents called their home. Grandpa had put Mike to work clearing out rocks from the shallow part of the lake right in front of their house. A dock with our grandparents' rowboat tied to it jutted out into the water. Off to the right the lake got really dark because of a steep drop-off. Grandma warned about that spot, relaying a story about how someone had drowned there years earlier. By the shore in that area, there were a bunch of reeds growing up out of the water. It looked spooky, like a 'creatures from the black lagoon' location. Mike shared about the great time he had exploring that lake and two adjoining ones on his last trip there.

We spent the rest of the afternoon reminiscing about old times and relating about school experiences and our girlfriends. We asked our grandparents if we could use their phone to call them later that evening. After dinner Mike went first. He took the phone, which was on a long extension cord, and went into the other room for some privacy. He talked a whopping thirty-five minutes to his girlfriend before coming back out.

"Mike, I done thought you got married, lived your life, and retired already."

"I really miss Colleen," my love-struck buddy replied.

"Long distance calls aren't cheap. I hope Grandpa and Grandma don't mind."

"Don't worry, they're cool."

I went into the vacated room and called Shari. Her mom answered.

"Hi Mrs. Lutz. Can I please talk with Shari?"

"Shari's not here right now," she replied.

"Okay, would you please tell her I'll call back later tonight?"

"Mark, Shari won't be back until tomorrow evening."

"Oh, where's she at?"

"Shari went on an overnight scuba-diving outing."

"Who'd she go with?" I questioned.

There was an awkward moment of silence before her reply. "Her scuba-diving club."

"Hmm, sounds like she's lovin' it. Will you tell her I'll call her in a couple days?" She said yes and our conversation ended. I had a weird feeling about this. I went back out into the living room.

"That sure was an economy call," Mike said.

"Just keepin' it short to give you more time to talk to your sweetheart, little buddy." I changed the subject to our upcoming canoe trip. We talked awhile longer and called it a night.

The next day Mike and I wanted to head in to town. We were anxious to pick up and pay for the canoe we'd ordered. There were other supplies we also needed to procure for our three-week expedition. Grandpa was going to give us a ride. We piled into his old blue Chevy truck and took off for town. The only thing was, Grandpa made a right turn and headed down a road away from town. After driving for a bit I began to wonder where we were going. Grandpa was getting older but he still seemed mentally sharp, not one to get confused.

"Grandpa, did we miss the turn-off to Ely?" I questioned. Grandpa smiled. "Just hold your horses, boys. I've got a little surprise for you."

Mike and I looked at each other. What was Grandpa up to? Before long we made a turn off the paved road and headed into the woods down a dirt road. The sun filtered through the trees. Then we came to a bright clearing with a log cabin house.

"Where are we, Grandpa?" Mike asked.

"Hang on. I want you boys to meet a friend of mine."

Out of the house emerged a weathered-skinned older gentleman wearing a flannel shirt and moccasins. "Bill, how you doing?" he greeted our Grandpa with a hug.

"I'm doing well, Chief. I'd like you to meet my two grandsons."

"I've heard about you two adventurous young men." And he invited us into his house.

We walked into what he called his Great Room. On the walls hung trophies from this man's life. Among his treasures were an elk head, a moose head, a ten-point buck, and a blue marlin. Turns out this fellow was quite the outdoorsman. When we asked about the blue marlin, he laughed and told us that it wasn't from around there, that he'd caught it on a fishing trip off the coast of Florida. Grandpa told us his proper title was Chief Running Bear, but that he was quite a wild one in his youth and had been nicknamed Chief Run Amuck.

Wanting to impress the Chief with his newly learned Indian word, Mike said, "Boozhoo."

"Are you Ojibwa?" the Chief asked. His smile had been replaced by a look of concern.

"No sir," Mike answered politely.

"Where did you learn that word?"

"Mark's uncle taught it to us after researching this area. It means hello."

"Many moons ago the Ojibwa chased my people, the Sioux, out of this area," the Chief explained. "The fighting lasted many years. The Ojibwa traded beaver skins for rifles with French trappers. That gave them an unfair advantage. Of course, that was then and this is now, and you're not one of them." The smile returned to the Chief's face.

He then brought us out to his garage and opened the door.

"Well, what do you think?" he asked. Parked there, was a beautiful sixteen-foot birchbark canoe.

"That's a great-looking canoe," Mike said. "Do you canoe a lot?"

"Used to," said the Chief. "My great-grandfather, a Dakota Sioux, built it back in the 1890s. It's been passed down in my family from generation to generation. It's had a number of repairs, and about five years ago it got a complete overhaul. And now it just sits here."

"That's a shame," I said. "A boat like that should grace the waters."

"My thought exactly. A boat like this should grace the waters," the Chief agreed.

"Well?" Grandpa asked smiling.

Mike and I looked at each other and replied simultaneously, "Well, what?"

"Would you boys like to use this canoe for your adventure?"

"Wow, would we!" I answered. "But, oh my goodness, what if something happened to it? We'd be sick!"

"Not to worry," said the Chief, "I'm giving it to you."

"You're going to give us this canoe?" Mike and I responded together, totally blown away by this man's generosity.

"Yes, I'm giving you this canoe. I'm the sole surviving member of my family and I'm not going to be doing any more canoeing. A boat like this begs to be on the water. Who am I to deny its request?"

I sat in the back of Grandpa's truck to brace the canoe while we drove back to his house. Mike kept peering through the back window with a Cheshire cat smile cemented on his face. We were two happy campers. We dropped the canoe off at the house and then headed into town. This time Grandpa made the right turn and we did end up in Ely. Main Street was loaded with canoe/camping outfitters, but of course, Ely is the canoe/camping capitol of the world. We found our shop, cancelled the purchase order for the canoe we had on hold, and then bought all the needed supplies for our trip. Their outfitter helped us plot out a canoe route. He said it would be challenging but thought we looked up to the task. There was no argument from us.

Once back at 'The Dove' we put on our newly acquired coonskin caps purchased in town and then went out canoeing. The canoe glided through the water on Eagle's Nest Lake as we paddled. With our hats on we felt like two Davey Crocketts on the wild frontier. We were pioneers exploring new territory. We were the Lewis and Clark of the modern age. The only difference right now was that, after our practice runs, we were able to come back to a nice cozy home and get refreshed. Five days from now, however, the rubber was going to meet the road, or more aptly for us, the birch was going to hit the water. We would begin roughing it on our three-week canoeing trek into the wild. We were born to be wild. Gee, that sounds like an idea for another song.

Just then a big fish brushed up alongside our canoe.

"Get a load of the size of that walleye!" Mike exclaimed.

"Get outta here. You wouldn't know the difference between a walleye and a barracuda," I responded.

"No, really, last time I was here Grandpa taught me about the different types of fish around this area: the small mouth bass, the lake trout, the northern pike, and as we just saw, the walleye."

"That's cool. Maybe you can teach me."

"For sure. And you know what's amazing?" Mike asked.

"No, what?"

"That walleye we just saw a moment ago," he paused, then grinning suspiciously went on, "is the same one I saw last summer when I was out here in Grandpa's rowboat."

"No way. How could you tell?" I asked, knowing all too well the answer.

"He winked at me."

We both busted out laughing. This was going to be a killer canoe trip.

The following day we went to church with our grandparents. Grandma was hyper-religious. You almost couldn't get a sentence out of her without a reference to the Lord. Sometimes it was annoying, but she was very sincere. I knew that she prayed for her children and grandchildren every day. It was easy for me to understand her need for prayer raising four boys and a girl, especially since I knew what my dad and his brothers were like. It's unfortunate that my dad was no longer with us. His heart attack and subsequent death two years earlier left quite a void in my life. I loved my dad. With the exception of me having to take a semester off from college, I'm sure he would have been proud of what Mike and I were undertaking.

After church we went out to eat and then returned to The Dove. We planned to spend the rest of the afternoon relaxing and enjoying the serenity of the lake. But first I had to make a phone call.

"Hi," Shari answered expectantly. She got it on one ring.

"Hi Shari, how are you?" I asked. There was a moment of hesitation before her reply. I got the feeling it wasn't my call she'd been so eagerly awaiting.

"Oh… Mark. Hi. Mom… mom said you were going to be calling. How's your trip going?" she responded, stumbling over her words, like something else was on her mind.

"The trip's going great! This place is like Eden on earth. It's so beautiful. One of my grandpa's friends gave us a canoe. How cool is that? We start our canoe trip in a few days and we'll be back in San Diego in about a month. How are you doing?"

"I'm doing fine."

"Okay, what you been up to? How was your overnight adventure with the scuba-diving club?" I asked.

"Scuba-diving club? Oh... oh that. It was fun."

"How are your scuba-diving lessons going?"

"Mark, I'm sorry, but I really don't have time to talk now. I'm supposed to be somewhere, but it's been nice talking to you."

"Yeah, it's been nice talking to you too." And that was it. Not really what I expected. I kept getting the feeling that Shari wasn't being straight with me. And then that dream about Shari falling for a scuba guy replayed in my head.

I went outside and sat on the porch swing and pondered our conversation. Grandma, sensing that something was up, came out and sat down beside me.

"Do you want to talk?" she asked. "You look a little bothered by something."

"I don't know, it's my girlfriend."

"What about her?"

"I don't know, Grandma, but I get this feeling like our relationship is about over. We seem to be going in different directions. At one time we even talked about getting married, but then issues started coming up."

"I know, your mother has talked to me about it."

"Oh, she has, has she?"

"Yes, we've talked about it and prayed about it because we want the best for your life. If this girl isn't right for you there will be another."

I perked right up. "Grandma, there's this girl in Boise, Idaho."

"Oh, there is, is there?"

"Yes, and she's gorgeous, and so much fun to be with. Mike and I stopped and saw her on our way here. And guess what Grandma?"

"What?"

"Grandma, I think she's in love with me."

"Mark, what are we going to do with you?"

"Keep praying, I guess." I grinned.

"By the way, what faith is this girl?"

"Oh, Grandma," I jumped up, "thanks, it's been nice talking with you."

I went back inside. Mike was on the phone in the other room. After another wallet-busting lengthy talk, my smiling starry-eyed buddy re-entered our world. In his case, absence really did seem to make the heart grow fonder. For myself, I definitely was not feeling the same.

"Mike, are you sure you still want to do the canoe trip?" I asked. "You know we won't be home for another month."

"Wouldn't miss it. Colleen is so excited to see pictures and hear about our adventure. I wouldn't want to disappoint her. I'm her knight in shining armor, her astronaut hoisting a flag on the moon, her ..."

"Mike, I get the picture."

"Hey, buddy, are you all right?" Mike asked. "You sound a little down."

"I'm okay. It's just Shari. I get the feeling I'm being replaced by a scuba-diving instructor with a boat. Before we left on our trip I was sensing that this could be it for us. Our interests were going in different directions. Then there's the faith issue and now this lengthy time apart. Who knows? Maybe a little jealousy is raising its head. Maybe it's just that I want to be the one calling the shots."

"Maybe, and maybe you're simply imagining this stuff with Shari, you dreamer. Are you sure you don't want to head back to San Diego early?"

"No way! I can't wait for our canoe trip, wouldn't miss it for the world. I just asked for your sake."

Chapter Eight

In the Blink of an Eye

Three days later, under a beautiful cloud-free sky, we loaded up
Grandpa's truck and he drove us to our starting point. This time I sat
up front with Grandpa and watched Mike while he held the canoe steady
in the back. We crossed those old railroad tracks, once used to ship iron-
ore down to Lake Superior before the mines were closed, and then made
a right onto Highway 1 towards town. Once in Ely we took the Fernberg
Road back out of town to the northeast, made a left turn down a forested
gravel road, and at its end, 'voila', Moose Lake.

Moose Lake is a popular starting point for canoe trips. It leads into
the protected Boundary Waters Canoe Area (BWCA), one million acres
of pristine unadulterated wilderness. Our adventure was going to take
us on a big loop which extended from there up into Canada's Quetico
National Park, another million acres of protected territory. Mike and I
were going to have Grandpa return to this spot in three weeks to pick
us up. I got out of the truck and Mike jumped out of the back. Just then
a park ranger approached. He looked eerily similar to the ranger at Mt.
Shasta and the caretaker at the cemetery. He too was very tall and fair-
skinned. And then, like the others, there were those deep intense eyes.

"Hi, boys, what you up to?" he asked.

Mike answered, "We're going canoeing."

"So I see. How far you going and for how long?"

Mike detailed our trip.

"That's quite a challenging venture you're undertaking," the ranger commented. "Hmm. Un-der-tak-ing, sounds like undertaker, makes you think, doesn't it? How much experience you boys have?"

Mike continued, "We've practiced on our grandpa's lake." Grandpa nodded. "And my cousin and I have backpacked together several times."

"In other words, not much," the ranger said with a concerned look on his face. "We've lost several people this year, one a seasoned canoeist who drowned in one of the falls off of Basswood River. You are going into the wilderness, you know. That word starts with wild for good reason."

"Sir, we get what you're saying," I said. "We'll take your warning and be careful. Our trip has been well-planned. And it helps that we're both in great shape."

"My grandsons will do just fine," Grandpa said confidently sticking up for us. "They remind me of me when I was young. I canoed. I fished. You may have even seen my picture on a billboard in Minneapolis promoting fishing."

"Can't say that I have," the ranger responded without interest.

"Caught a record-sized walleye," Grandpa beamed.

"There ya go, Mr. Ranger, sir. Not to worry, it's in our blood," Mike said looking proudly at Grandpa.

The ranger further cautioned us about the possibility of extreme weather changes, then said as he looked directly at Mike, "You gotta watch out for Mother Nature 'cause she can take you out in the blink of an eye." He turned and started walking away.

"Whoa!! Mr. Ranger, sir," Mike called out after him. "Why were you looking at me? You don't happen to have a brother who works at Mt. Shasta, do you? "

The ranger looked back over his shoulder. The sunlight ignited a dazzling fiery sparkle in his eyes. "We're all brothers," he said. "You, me, that fellow 'cross the lake, we're all brothers." Then, gently stomping his boot on the ground for effect, he finished with, "We all have to take care of Mother Earth."

"We will," I said. "And don't worry about my little buddy here," I grinned while playfully hitting Mike in the shoulder, "I personally guarantee his safe return."

Mike just looked at me and shook his head.

The ranger disappeared into the dense woodlands.

"Come on you hooligans, let's get a move on it. Stand around here much longer and your boots are going to start growing moss on them," Grandpa nudged.

We unloaded Grandpa's truck and brought everything down by the lakeshore. Loons were calling out to one another in the distance. The lake was like glass, a mirror, the reflection of the shoreline with its forest of trees. We loaded our gear and food, all packed in water-tight bags in case we should capsize, and secured it all to the canoe. A few other canoeists had begun to arrive.

"Shove off," Grandpa encouraged. "I'll be back here three weeks from today to pick you up."

Mike and I pushed our beautiful gear-laden birch-bark canoe into the water, hopped onboard, and began paddling. The canoe sliced into the mirror that was the lake, shattering its surface and leaving small ripples in its wake. We turned and waved our paddles good-bye one last time as Grandpa slowly shrank in size while watching from the shore left behind. We were on our way.

We paddled and coasted and paddled and coasted. This was going to be great for our arms and upper bodies. My muscles were already enjoying the exercise. The sun beamed down on us with a smile, much like I envisioned my dad was. He'd have been so proud. 'Life is good,' I thought.

I was wearing my baby-blue fisherman's hat and prescription sunglasses. I remember the hat getting me into hot water my senior year in high school. Our tennis coach had acquired new white uniforms for the team and told me I couldn't wear it in competition anymore. I told him I couldn't play without it. Then I wouldn't be playing, he informed. He said my hat clashed with the team uniforms. He over-emphasized the word team and added something about unity. "But coach, it brings me luck and helps keep the sweat out of my eyes," I'd pleaded. We dickered a while more before he finally gave in. He was a good coach. And I loved my hat. Mike wasn't wearing one, but he did have on his dark sunglasses. They made him look like a movie-star.

The first couple days we canoed vigorously to escape civilization. After Moose Lake we encountered a series of smaller lakes. There were several short portages we made from lake to lake. Carrying our packs on our backs and the canoe overhead on our shoulders made for a hefty workout. Rugged terrain didn't make it any easier.

Canoeing our way up Knife Lake there was one stop we didn't want to miss. Somewhere on this long lake was an island of pine trees where a lady named Dorothy Molter lived. She was famous in these parts for her homemade root beer. We were told it was quite good. After a few days in the wilderness we thought it would be a refreshing treat.

Upon reaching that island, we steered our canoe into her three-tier parking structure and gave the valet a couple bucks to watch it. Confused you, hey? Just kidding. We pulled the canoe ashore and set out to find Dorothy's cabin. A group of mallards had congregated near the landing, probably to discuss their upcoming trip south. Chipmunks scurried about, cheeks full, gathering food to store in their burrows. Winter was fast approaching and those in the animal kingdom were making preparations. We found several cabins but no 'root beer lady'. We set out exploring. On the east side of the island we discovered another smaller island only a hundred feet away. It was connected by a short rustic pier. We crossed over and there she was, an elderly white-haired woman living in a large tent-like cabin. No electricity, no phone, no television, not much of anything but wilderness, no kidding.

"Welcome boys!" she greeted. "I'll bet you're awfully thirsty."

"Matter of fact we are. And we hear you have the best root beer in these parts," Mike flattered.

"The only root beer in these parts," Dorothy laughed. "I guess that would make it the best. Nearest town's 36 miles away as the whooping crane flies."

"Don't you get lonely or scared way out here?" Mike asked.

"Nope. I get plenty of visitors during the summer season and even a few during the winter."

"You honestly don't get scared here?" he reiterated in disbelief.

"Nope. Lived here 38 years. The only thing that's scared me is the government. They tried to force me to move when this lake became part of the Boundary Waters Canoe Area. This is now federally protected wilderness."

"How can they do that?" I questioned.

"Inquisitive boys, you two. I'll bet you drove your parents nuts."

"My mom blames my fourth-grade teacher," I replied. "Mr. Jones had us question darn near everything. Insanity did become a possibility for her."

"The answer to your inquiry is this. The government was using something called eminent domain. That's where they can trump our personal rights if they determine a higher and better use of the land 'for the people' as a whole."

"So why you still here?"

"'The people,'" Dorothy smiled broadly. "Many canoe enthusiasts protested loudly. The government conceded. Myself and one other fellow are allowed to live in this vast territory until we die."

"You rebel woman, you," Mike joshed. "You beat the system. I'm surprised you didn't mysteriously get killed by a runaway moose."

Dorothy shared stories of her fascinating life with us. She was a nurse and periodically had to go back to the big city for continuing education to keep certified. Those trips must've felt strange to someone also dubbed 'the loneliest woman in the world'. During the winter she had huge blocks of ice cut from the lake and stored them in a primitive shelter for refrigeration. She told us it usually lasted through most of the summer. Mike and I had a nice visit, and of course, drank some of Dorothy's tasty root beer. She showed us a good site to camp so we fished a little, ate a fried trout dinner from our catch, and stayed the night. And what was on our menu for breakfast the next morning, leftover trout. Mmm!

North of Dorothy's isle was another stop she told us about. It was a spot called Thunder Point. She said it was a 150' rise which at the top had a spectacular panoramic view of the surrounding territory. It involved a rigorous quarter-mile uphill hike. Once there, we were awed by the sight. It was breathtaking! One could see for miles and miles. We sat there for an hour basking in the beauty of God's creation, the sheer genius of it all. It was perfect. Suddenly a city-dweller-type thought came over me.

"Hey, Mike, what if while we're up here enjoying this view somebody takes our canoe with all our gear in it?"

"Ain't gonna happen," he replied confidently. "Besides, we haven't seen another soul all day."

"Yeah, but *what if* someone did?" I questioned.

"Canoeists, outdoorsmen, don't do that sort of thing. There's an honor code," Mike assured.

"Sez who?" I asked like the devil's advocate.

"Sez me," Mike answered, but I could tell he was starting to think about it. "We should get going," he suggested.

We started back down to the landing. Our hike back definitely had more urgency to it. I told Mike about a time I got ripped off two years earlier. I'd just returned from a skiing trip to Mammoth Mountain. It was 2am and I was dead tired. I brought my skis and poles into my house and was going to get the rest of my stuff in the morning. The car was locked. That next morning when I went out to my car I noticed my wing window was broken. A sickening feeling wrenched my gut. Sure enough, my case, my very large case, which held my 8-track tapes, 36 of them in all, was missing. And it was full! I was infuriated, seeing blood red. If I had caught the thief that day I might have killed him. I was so angry. I felt so violated. I never did find that thief. What were Mike and I going to find when we got back down to the lakeshore?

Our canoe and all our gear.

"You idiot," my buddy voiced with relief, seeing that everything was still there. "You got me all worked up for nothing."

More lakes, more portages, more pan-fried fish, more of nature consumed our days. It was quite fulfilling. There was more wildlife too. We saw a moose standing in a shallow marshy spot by the shore of one lake. Another time we spotted an otter. Neither seemed very concerned with our presence. Peace reigned, or did the serenity of this place lull one into a false sense of security? One of those days, after we'd found a nice campsite for the night, Mike went exploring. He was about a hundred feet away when he called out to me in a rather hushed voice laced with distress.

"Mark, I've got a black bear staring right at me. What should I do?"

"Don't panic, stay calm," I warned. "Stare back, and whatever you do, don't run. He's faster than you. Is he big?"

"I don't know, medium sized I guess."

"Okay, I'll tell you. Raise your arms over your head. Make yourself look really big, then start growling loudly."

"You're kidding. You tryin' to get me killed?"

"No. Just do it. Trust me."

"Grr," came a tentative effort from my buddy as he lifted his arms. The bear raised up on his back haunches and baring his teeth growled back.

"Mark, he looks hungry," came a squeamish plea for help.

"Growl louder. Jump up and down."

"GRrr."

"Louder!! Like your life depends on it! Think Grizzly!"

"GRRR! GRRRRR!!!"

The bear sized up Mike, then went back down on all fours and scampered off into the woods. Mike walked back towards me and sat down. "Don't talk to me. I just need to relax."

After a few minutes Mike looked noticeably relieved.

"You need to change your shorts?" I asked.

"Very funny. Phew! For a minute there I thought I was a goner, that I was going to become a gourmet meal."

"Gourmet. Now look who's the comedian. Tube steak at best. Maybe a Big Mike at a fast food joint. I'm just glad you didn't get mauled. You're irreplaceable."

"Yeah, or you'd have to finish this trip solo, huh? Seriously though," Mike said with gratitude, "thanks for the advice. How'd you know what to do?"

"I didn't."

"You didn't?!"

"Well, not really. I think I might have seen something on a nature show or read something somewhere."

"You think you may have. Dude, I could've been killed. 'Trust me'!"
I smiled.

"You're messin' with me, aren't you?" Mike wanted to know.

"Am I? ...I really do think I heard that somewhere. It worked, didn't it? What else were you going to do?"

That night, before sacking out in our sleeping bags, I asked Mike if he knew that he snored. He said he'd never been told that and wanted to know why I asked. I moved my bag a little farther from his before answering. "I think I read somewhere that bears are attracted to snoring."

"You trying to drive me crazy? Won't work."

I smiled again.

And Mike slept with one eye open that night.

Up to this point we'd enjoyed navigating several smaller rapids. There's a thrill you get when going fast, living on the edge, testing your mental and physical abilities. There's the sound of rushing water adding intensity to the experience. Danger, danger! It cries out, getting your heart to beat faster and your adrenaline to start pumping. Mike was enthralled with this part of our journey. Perhaps that explained his love of surfing. The powerful ocean, with its crashing waves and strong rip currents, also had that element.

Canoeing up Kawnipi Lake we had a situation develop that even Mike didn't relish. Our map had the word DANGEROUS! spelled out in bold red type at one spot. There was also an arrow just below that spot pointing to a portage. We were paddling along when our canoe started to pick up speed. Both of us were well aware of what the map said. We tried to get closer to the left bank but the way to it was clogged with big rocks jutting out of the water and fallen dead trees. Our canoe was picking up more speed. The sound of fast water grew. Had we missed our portage?

"Mike," I yelled from behind.

"I know," he shouted back, "I'm looking."

There was panic in his voice. I was right there with him on that. I'd heard about people dying getting swept over falls. I'd heard about the drownings, the mangled bodies, the broken-up canoes. We were too young to die. We still had a whole lot of living to do. We had this trip to finish. 'Grandpa'd kill us if we didn't come back alive,' I thought. We were really racing along now, caught in a current of doom. My heart wanted to beat its way out of my chest, to escape. The sound of fast water was now crushing.

"Mike," I yelled again.

"I know," he shouted back once more. "Maybe we missed… No, no, wait, I SEE IT!"

There it was, off to the left up ahead, our missing portage, our salvation, our path to avoid destruction. We steered hard left and found clear passage to the shore. Once safe on that shore we sat down and we busted out laughing, and we laughed, and we laughed some more. There was a euphoric sense of relief. This wasn't the first time. Hopefully it would be our last. I feared that our good fortune in dodging disaster might eventually run out. We were tempting fate.

This portage took us down a trail to the base of the waterfall. It was treacherous, full of overgrowth, a muddy path with roots trying to ensnare our every step. Twist an ankle or break a leg here and one is in a heap of trouble. There are no emergency care centers around the next corner. Aware of this, Mike and I cautiously planted each step we took. We made it safely to the bottom. A fine mist floated in the air. A constant roar filled our ears, the sound of cascading water crashing into the pool beside us. We portaged around a couple more waterfalls we encountered on this segment of our journey. The land was beautiful but rugged. Traversing it was tough.

Up until this point we'd had great weather, but now it was beginning to get breezy. Change was brewing in the air. Some scout clouds began to appear, searching for a good place to attack. Soon they were followed by an army of war clouds. The sky blackened. Lightning flashed, cracking the darkness. Thunder boomed. We no sooner hunkered down in our tent when the barrage began. Large raindrops, like little cannonballs, pelted the earth around us. We were deluged in a torrent of rain for a day and a half. By the time the bombardment ended and the sky cleared we were antsy to be on our way. There's only so many hands of poker, or games of solitaire, or writing in a journal that one can bear before going stir crazy.

With blue skies overhead and the sun reappearing, Mike and I continued. Cooler temperatures had us dressing more warmly. The next few days we worked our way across the most northern part of our trip in Canada. One thing we noticed is that our portages were more difficult here. For that matter, they had been ever since we crossed the border. The trails were better maintained on the United States side. Perhaps the Canadians wanted to keep their park as wild as they could.

One afternoon, a couple weeks into our canoeing trip, Mike and I were in the middle of a lake fishing for dinner. Nothing new about that. We weren't having any luck though. I was surprised because I had on old faithful, a lure that seldom came up empty. It was a gold and silver spinner with three fake salmon eggs attached. I loved watching the unsuspecting fish follow the lure in and when it could no longer resist the temptation, take a bite. Dinner is served. A slight wind started blowing and a few clouds came into sight as we patiently waited.

"Mike, you know why they call this Lake Sturgeon?"

"Probably named after some guy named Sturgeon," he guessed.

"Nope. Guess again."

"How 'bout after someone who likes mixed drinks."

"Mixed drinks?" I was puzzled by that response.

"Yeah, stir gin. Get it?" Mike grinned.

"Good answer, but wrong again. You evidently don't have a clue."

"Okay, professor, I give up. Why do they call this Lake Sturgeon?"

"It's named after a bird found only in this part of the world. Actually, two birds, the stork and the carrier pigeon. They mated and created a freakish looking off-shoot called the sturgeon. They have long white beaks like the stork and short tiny legs and feet like the pigeon. You rarely see them because they're so shy. I bet that's 'cause they're embarrassed about their over-proportioned beaks."

"You really think I'm buying this?" Mike chuckled. "Tell me more. Let's see if your nose grows."

"You want more, I've got more. They're never seen in the city because they don't balance well on window sills or small ledges. Their beaks make them top heavy so they tend to topple over. You oftentimes see them with scuffed beaks, especially the lazier ones, those that fail to keep their heads up. It's similar to somebody dragging their feet when walking. And lastly, another reason for their humiliation, unlike their relatives, is their inability to deliver anything. Carrier pigeons deliver notes and storks deliver babies."

"Dude, what mental ward did you escape from?"

"Look! There's one now," I quickly exclaimed glancing over Mike's shoulder, pointing behind him.

Mike turned to look.

"I guess it's the same ward as you," I answered.

The truth is, Lake Sturgeon was really named after a fish, not a bird. It's a large lake and we were still in the middle of it. The weather seemed to be deteriorating rapidly. We reeled in our lines and began paddling into the wind at a slight angle towards the shore. It was a long way off, maybe as much as a mile. The lake got choppy. Small whitecaps were beginning to form. The wind started gusting which felt like cold slaps to the face. It began to drizzle, hiding the shoreline from sight. Waves grew. Our forward progress was grinding to a halt. The situation looked forbidding.

"Mark, I think we should retreat," my suddenly sane friend suggested.

"I agree. I hate going backwards, but at this rate we aren't going to make it."

"We can use the waves to our advantage," Mike said grinning mischievously.

'Uh-oh!' I thought. 'What could he be thinking at a time like this'. I got the feeling he was up to something nutty. We turned our canoe around and paddled. One of the larger waves caught our canoe and began propelling it along. Next thing I knew, Mike was standing.

"Mike! Sit down!" I yelled. "What the heck are you doing?"

"Sorry. I just had to try it."

"Try what? Getting killed?"

"No. Catch a wave and you're sittin' on top of the world. We're in Canada, can't get much closer to the top than that."

"Ooh, right now I could shoot The Beatles for writing those lyrics."

"It wasn't The Beatles."

"I meant The Bee Gees."

"It wasn't them either. It was The Beach Boys," Mike said. I smirked. "You knew that too, didn't you? You messing with me again?"

"Look who's messin' with who. Don't scare me like that anymore," I warned.

We made it back to shore all right and spent the next day waiting out this latest onslaught of inclement weather. Rapids, waterfalls, and now the waves on this lake had seasoned us two rookie canoeists. The outfitter that mapped out our route said it would be testy. And it had been just that. He also thought we'd be up to the task, that we appeared hardy enough. We were proving him right, Grandpa too.

This trip strengthened the bond of friendship Mike and I had. We laughed. We kidded each other in good fun. We shared our lives, our past experiences, our dreams for the future, our concerns. We were responsible young men, or boys if you went by the opinion of the 'root beer' lady and that zombie park ranger. Whichever, we were confident, hard-working, fun-loving guys. We had enjoyed our trip immensely but now it was time. Time for what? Time to get home. We wanted to get back to real life, to work, to school, to our families, and to our girlfriends. Mike was sorely missing Colleen. Maybe that's what put him in the craze that had him standing in our canoe.

As for me and Shari, I missed her but... Hmm, was that it? Did I simply miss her butt? How shallow that would be. No, there's a lot more to her than that. Something else was going on with us. I needed to know. It felt like we were dangling. I was unsure and I don't like uneasy feelings, loose ends, unfinished business. If things weren't going to work out for us I was ready to move on. Like the gold rushers of old from the early part of our trip, I'd already done some prospecting. I'd staked a claim. What would I find though, the real stuff or fool's gold?

The next day was stormy and furious. When the bad weather had mostly cleared out we resumed. After Lake Spurgeon came the Maligne River. It was put-on-your-seatbelt fast, especially towards the middle. We're talking e-ticket, rollercoaster ride fast. It was exciting. I think Mike must've thought he'd died and gone to heaven. He was so elated. This was a great way to start the last leg of our journey.

On the following day more heavy-laden clouds appeared. It got blustery once again. This time though, the temperature kept dropping and dropping like a lead balloon. Snowflakes began to fall. It was time to find a place to camp.

Mike looked back at me. "More rapids coming up. You a player?" he asked excitedly. He was hooked on their exhilaration. He was an addict.

"Mike, the weather, we should set up camp."

"Oh, come on. You only live once. How about we set up camp right after these? Wha' da you say?"

"I guess," I said hesitantly. "I'm a player if you are." I too got a rush out of running rapids but wasn't quite as fearless as my buddy. These looked more treacherous.

Our canoe began to pick up speed. We touched paddles in a high five manner.

"Cowabunga!" Mike yelled.

"Banzai!" I hollered back.

The river wanted to take control. It was bucking like a wild bronco in its effort to throw us. It needed to be broken in, to be tamed. We were the two canoeing cowboys to do it.   "To the left," Mike yelled out. We both dug our paddles in, our canoe swerved,   narrowly missing a big boulder.

"Right, right!" he shouted, as another one quickly appeared. We dug into the right only we got caught in an overpowering eddy. It spun us around backwards. Frantically we tried to get the canoe turned back around but it was too late. There was a slight drop and another giant rock. We crashed into it at a forty-five degree angle. There was a big spray of water and then the canoe lurched, launching both Mike and me into the rapidly moving river. I grabbed on to a low hanging branch. Mike was right behind me. He appeared rather lethargic and I quickly caught him by his arm to keep him from floating off.

"I gotcha, buddy," I yelled over the roar of the river.

"I don't feel so good," he replied weakly. Blood was spilling from a deep gash in his head. He evidently had hit the rock.

"Mike, not to worry. You're going to be all right. I'll get you out of this," I assured. His eyes looked pained.

'Dang this water is freezing,' I thought as I looked to the nearby shore. 'How am I going to get us onto the bank?'

The water was rushing. My hand was going numb. What was I to do? I felt stuck. I looked back at Mike.

"I gotta know," he said with lots of effort.

Thinking this is no time for small talk, I responded anyway, "You gotta know what?"

"The poker, …with the girls. …would you have?"

"You've got to be kidding."

"Would you have?" he gasped.

"No," I answered.

Mike grinned slightly. He seemed relieved. Then he went limp and his eyes became a lifeless blank stare.

"NO!" I cried out. "This can't be happening. Little buddy, we're invincible. Hang in there."

There was no response.

"N.O.O..O...O…..O!" I wailed.

Then my mind began messing with me. There in Mike's eyes stood, just like the grim reaper, the park ranger. He kept saying, "In the blink of an eye, in the blink of an eye, in the blink of an eye. I warned you."

"Ah, shut up you imp," I blurted out angrily.

"But you guaranteed, you guaranteed. Where's your guarantee now?" he taunted.

I closed my eyes for a moment to clear my mind and get free from my wicked tormentor. 'Maybe I'd hit my head too. Maybe I have a concussion. It would explain all this weirdness,' I thought. Things had happened so quickly. I reopened my eyes. Mike was gone. 'Oh crap! Where'd Mike go?' I panicked and let go of the branch. The current quickly carried me over the next hundred yards. This was not your friendly water-park ride. There were some hard hits and crashes, and then, at the end of my ride, I was forced underwater. When I resurfaced the river had died to calm.

Wet, cold, sore, and extremely exhausted, I somehow managed to get to shore and pull myself up an embankment. Snow was still falling, only harder now and it was starting to collect on the ground. Feeling like a frozen icicle, I looked downriver. There was no sign of Mike or our canoe. My heart and brain went into intense deliberation. I should go after Mike, maybe I can help him. You'd never make it, you're too weak. But he's my best friend, I can't just abandon him. Your best friend wouldn't want to see you dead too. What do you mean too? Maybe he's still alive. But you saw him die right in your grasp. Did I? You did. 'Oh, God,' I questioned, 'how can this be happening to me, to us?'

Reason won out in an irrational situation. At least try and save yourself. I had to choke back the tears as I scanned the area for shelter. Luckily, I spotted an overhang in the hillside and worked my way towards it. I was hurting, physically and emotionally. It felt like I'd just played a couple hours of contact football, without pads, and lost miserably. My head was ringing. And my heart was aching. I was totally beaten up.

Amazingly, a second piece of good fortune arrived when I got under the overhang. Lying around, like treasure from a sunken Spanish galleon, were a bunch of dead branches. Dead branches equal fuel for a fire and I knew I needed to warm up or I was a goner. I was shivering so hard I could hear my teeth chatter. I felt like my eyeballs were going to freeze in their sockets, using my skull like an ice tray. That's when I realized a third bit of good fortune. I'd lost everything I had except for a knife clipped to my belt and a small box of waterproof matches in a buttoned shirt pocket. I whittled off some woodchips from one of the branches, lit a match, and got a fire started. The fire blazed as I added more wood. I took off my waterlogged boots to dry them out. The heat felt great, but I continued to shake uncontrollably so I moved closer to the flames. At this moment even Hell and it's eternal fire didn't sound so bad. Just then my pantleg caught on fire. 'Oh crap!' I quickly backed away and snuffed it out. 'That's all I need to do now, make an ash out of myself.' I thought in an inane attempt at humoring myself. I was getting delirious.

My head, which had been ringing, turned to throbbing. It was like somebody was banging on a bass drum right next to my ear. BOOM! BOOM! BOOM! I threw another branch on the fire, only this one must've been damp because it sent up a big plume of smoke. The smoke collected under the overhang before wafting out. Immediately, hundreds, maybe even thousands of tiny white spiders began descending like paratroopers from above. I was creeped out! It felt like the whole top of my head was crawling. I went to brush it off. When my hand came down it was all bloody. Then I heard a noise behind me and quickly turned. There, embedded in the sandstone wall, was a rock. It looked like a giant eyeball. And there he was again in its midst, my tormentor.

"In the blink of an eye. ...I warned you. ...And you guaranteed. ... Where's your buddy now? ...Ha, ha, ha, ha, ...where's your guarantee now? ...You know, ...it's all your fault, ...it's all your fault, ...it's all........."

Drowning in guilt, I passed out.

Chapter Nine

Hooked with Looks

"It's all your fault. It's all your fault…"

"Okay, okay, I get it! Now leave me alone. Please leave me alone," I begged. Tears rolled down my cheeks. Then I felt a warm hand stroke my forehead and heard a familiar reassuring voice tell me that I was going to be all right. I opened my eyes. There was my mom. "Mom. What are you doing here?" I asked with a puzzled look. "Where am I? How'd I get here?"

"You're in the hospital."

"I can see that, but how'd I get here?"

"Your cousin, he saved your life," she answered.

"My cousin? No way." I thought back to our ordeal. "Mom, he died. I watched him die. It was awful! And …and it's all my fault."

"It's not your fault, son. Accidents happen. It's part of life."

"But…"

"No buts, dear. It's not your fault," Mom repeated firmly. "And Mike really did save your life."

"No way. How could he have?" I questioned. "I'm not kidding, I was holding onto him when he died. Then he slipped out of my grasp and was swept away. Please tell me it was only a nightmare."

My mom looked at me solemnly. "It wasn't a nightmare. I'm sorry, Mike is dead. His body was found downriver with your canoe. That's what alerted authorities to send out search parties to look for a missing person. So you see, in a way, that's how Mike saved your life."

"Mom, that's terrible. It's not fair. I should have died too. We were a team, we were in it together. And you can tell me it isn't, but I still feel like it's all my fault."

"Mark, it's not your fault," Mom said again as she leaned over and hugged me. "Your cousin wouldn't want you to feel that way. He'd definitely want you to be alive, to make him proud, to carry on the family name."

"Mom, but the way he looked at me, with pleading eyes, wanting my help, and I promised. I couldn't help him." I began to sob.

"It's okay, son. You're going to be all right," my mom consoled while holding me tight.

Nothing was said for the next few minutes.

"When is Mike's funeral?" I asked after regaining my composure. "If it's okay with Aunt Jean and the family, I'd really like to say something at it."

"That's not going to be possible."

"Sure it will. I doubt they'll mind."

"Son, Mike's funeral was last week."

"Last week?"

"Yes, last week. You've been in a coma for nine days."

"Nine days?" I wondered aloud.

"Yes, nine days. You had a lot of swelling on your brain so the neurologist kept you in an induced coma to aid your recovery and help prevent long-term damage."

"Oh, crap!" I exclaimed in disappointment. "I can't believe I missed his funeral again."

"What do you mean again?" Mom was confused.

"Mom, early on in our trip I had a dream. It felt so real. I dreamed we were hit by a drunk driver and Mike was killed and I missed his funeral because …" I stopped talking. My next thought shook me up.

"Mark, are you all right?" my mom asked with a worried look on her face.

"Mom. Tell me I'm not paralyzed."

"You're not paralyzed."

"You're not just saying that? You're not hiding something from me, are you?"

"Oh honey, I'm telling you the truth. Go ahead and move your legs, see for yourself," she told me.

I took a deep breath and mentally prepared myself for the worst, then, I moved my legs. 'Duh! Why didn't I think of that?' I thought. 'What an idiot.'

Well, I wasn't paralyzed. I just spooked myself out thinking that my dream may have been a premonition of things to come. I mean, hey, what was I to think? Mike's dead and I'm in the hospital. That's a little too close for comfort. I was relieved that I wasn't paralyzed, yet at the same time, it's strange, but I was sad that I hadn't died with my best friend. Two of the closest people in my life had died untimely deaths. My dad, and now Mike. 'Get close to Mark and start shopping for a headstone,' I thought.

The staff psychologist at the hospital strongly recommended that I get some counseling when I returned to San Diego. Mom assured him that I would. Me, I'm thinking, 'No way. I will work through this on my own. What do they think I am, weak-minded?' All I needed was to return to some normalcy, some stability in my life. I couldn't wait to see Shari again, to get one of her cuddly hugs. I realized that our relationship may have drifted apart, but right now I just wanted some of the same ol'. I was not ready for more change. Or should I be? Two days later I flew home to San Diego.

We've all heard, "There's no place like home." How true that is. As I walked up the sidewalk to the front door there were the philodendrons planted next to the brick-veneered front of our house. Once inside, there was the large ornate mirror mounted over the gold and green sofa. Hanging lamps my parents bought in Mexico hung in the corner. The pictures on the walls were the same. At the end of the hallway there was the same faded picture of me as an infant. I was wearing a diaper, laying on my stomach with my head raised looking around. Out of the kitchen came the familiar smell of Mom's hot-dish simmering on the stove. It's a concoction of macaroni noodles, hamburger, and tomato sauce. Mmm, mmm, good! Yes, normalcy.

Before I totally settled in, though, there was something that just couldn't wait. I dialed the phone on the kitchen wall. Shari answered.

"Hi, Shari, I'm back."

"Hi, Mark. I'm so sorry about your cousin."

"Me too."

"I went to his funeral."

"I couldn't be there," I responded apologetically.

"I know, I was told you were still in a coma."

"How was the service?"

"It was very moving. The church was packed. They even prayed for you."

"And, voila, here I am. I'd like to see you."

"I'd like to see you too," Shari replied. "We should talk."

"I can come right now," I suggested.

"That'd be fine. The sooner the better," she answered.

Yessiree! A little bit of talkin' and a whole lotta huggin' and a kissin'. I couldn't wait to see her. Then came the thought, 'Who am I trying to fool?'

"Hey, Mom, I'm going over to Shari's for a while. I'll be back later."

"Mark," came the concerned voice from across the kitchen, "There's something you ought to ..."

"Stop, Mom, I know what's going on. I'm not that dense." I hugged her, and on my way out told her to call Grandma if she was worried. I knew I was going to my own lynching.

Twenty minutes later I was ringing Shari's doorbell. She answered, stepped out on the front porch, and shut the door behind her. A pair of eyes glanced out the front window. They didn't belong to her brother. When I went to give Shari a hug and a kiss, she turned her head and took one on the cheek.

"How are you feeling?" she asked, looking up at the bandages on my head.

"I'm feeling fine. I survived. How 'bout you?"

"I'm doing well. Again, I'm really sorry about Mike."

"Life, and in this case death, happens. It can get crappy. I keep getting the feeling that Mike's death is my fault."

"Maybe you should see a therapist," Shari suggested.

"Not you too."

"Well, you should."

"I'll get over it."

"Mark, we need to talk," she insisted.

"Talk about what, your new boyfriend?"

"How'd you know?"

"I saw him peeking out the window. Not to worry about me, I've already got a new girl."

"How could you!?" she blurted out like I'd betrayed her.

"Shhh! You've got no room to talk. You've got a new guy. How could *you?*" I retaliated. "The question now is, can we still be friends? I'd like that if you would."

"No. My boyfriend wouldn't like that idea."

"But what about you?"

"It'd get awkward. I really don't want to upset him."

"He have a name?"

"Doesn't matter, does it?"

"Guess not. Wow. That's it. It's over. We had some fun, though, didn't we? I'll need my stereo back."

"I brought it back to your moms' last week."

I wished her well and waved good-bye to her boyfriend behind the curtain. He ducked out of sight. I got back in my car and sat there for a while contemplating everything that had just happened. Okay, I didn't really have a new girl yet, at least not officially. But I didn't feel like letting her one-up me. It was over. And we weren't even going to be friends. And to think that we had talked about marriage at one point. And not even be friends. That blew me away. There was such a finality to it. It felt like another death. It was depressing. I couldn't go home now feeling like this so I went by my friend Jake's house. He was home.

Jake loved to party. He was a party animal. I knew I could count on him to help cheer me up. It was also fitting because he was the one responsible for me meeting Shari in the first place. We made a stop at a liquor store on our way to the beach. Intending to drown my sorrows, I walked out with two six-packs. They must have thought I was at least twenty-one, or so I liked to think 'cause it made me feel grown up. Truth is they were probably more interested in profits and not too worried about losing their liquor license.

By the time we got to La Jolla Shores the sun was a fiery red ball sinking into the ocean. It too seemed to be drowning. We set up our lawn chairs in the sand. I pulled the tab off a can of beer and commenced drinking. Jake did likewise.

"Hey, Jake, you better watch out, you could be next."

"What do you mean?"

"What do you mean what do you mean? Isn't it obvious? Everything around me dies."

"Not me," he responded.

"Maybe not now, but you just wait and see."

"Mark, what's going on? You're one of the most positive, upbeat people I know."

"I killed my cousin."

"Get off it. You didn't kill anybody."

"Jake, I'm responsible. The trip was my idea, the canoeing part too."

"Did you hold a shotgun to Mike's head forcing him to go?"

"Well, no."

"Well, there you have it. It was his choice. It's on him. Hell, I would have liked to have gone on the trip with you."

"Yeah, then you'd be dead."

"Maybe, maybe not. At least I'd have died happy, enjoying life. Remember last year when you took me skiing at Mammoth. It was my first time and you coaxed me into trying some pretty gnarly runs."

I smiled devilishly, "Yeah, you fell a lot. I could've got you killed too." They were some awfully hard slopes for a beginner.

"But I survived. And when I fell, you encouraged me to get back up, dust myself off, and keep going. I improved. I'll tell you, that was one of the best times of my life. I'll bet Mike would say so too."

Suddenly I was overwhelmed with emotion. There was Mike's death. Then I got thinking about my dad and his heart attack and how much I missed him. Dad could've helped me get a handle on my life. And finally, there was my break-up with Shari. Death, death, death. Well, it was depressing. I heard what Jake was saying but I wasn't buying it.

"Those tears?" Jake asked.

"I'm just leaking beer," I answered.

"Here, have another. Chill out."

Neither one of us spoke for a long while. Darkness blanketed our view of the ocean. All that could be heard was the crash of waves breaking and the softer sound of water rushing ashore and then slowly retreating. There was a lulling peacefulness to it.

"You heard about Shari, didn't you?" I started up again.

"When you picked me up you told me. Get over it. We're sitting in front of a great big ocean."

"So?"

"So! There are lots of fish in it if you get my drift."

"I get it." I sat there quietly pondering life before saying anything else. "Jake, do you remember a girl from high school named Chelsea?"

"Yeah, she was cute."

"Well, she's more than cute now. She's a knockout!" I perked up. "Mike and I saw her on our trip."

"Hmm," Jake grinned. "Sounds like you've already been fishing."

"She'd be a prize catch. Do you remember why she moved?"

"Not really. It was a little strange. It was right in the middle of our junior year. One day she was there, the next she was gone."

"That is weird. Hey, how'd you like to do some skiing in Idaho over winter break?" I asked.

"Why Idaho?" Jake joshed. "Big Bear or Mammoth would be much closer."

"You know, you're right. Did I tell you about Chelsea's hot-looking friend?"

"I'll start packing tonight."

"His name is Bruce."

"Very funny."

We began planning our trip to Boise. I was going to drive. Had to. Jake didn't have a car. I didn't mind, I loved my car. It was a baby-blue 1965 Ford Fairlane with custom tuck 'n' roll swirly ocean-blue naugahyde seats. It had an outstanding 8-track stereo system in it with both front and rear speakers. Quadraphonic! Rock and roll! And did I ever think it was the cat's meow with the ski racks on top. I took great pride in my car, bought and paid for with lots of hard work. Jake and I finished our beers and then I drove him home.

When I awoke in my bed the next morning I couldn't remember how I got there. 'What's that all about?' I wondered.

Yes, what was that all about? And it wouldn't be the last time. It wasn't really about my dad. He had lived a rather stressful life. Besides running his own business, he was president of the town council and very active in politics. He also was involved in Little League baseball and helped create a local girls softball league. It was always meeting, meeting, meeting, go go, go. He was a racehorse that didn't know the words slow down. Gaining weight didn't bode well for him either because one day, at age 36, his ticker gave out. I loved my dad, miss him dearly, but I never felt responsible for his death.

Then there was Shari and the demise of that relationship, but it really wasn't about that either. Our relationship already seemed to have run its course. The writing was on the wall. The religion dilemma especially had been looming large. With Mike's death our breakup was simply bad timing. I wasn't too keen on having to deal with so much change all at once. There was a bright side to this, though, in that it left me completely unchained and free to chase after Chelsea. And that looked very promising.

So what was it about? It was about Mike. I felt responsible for his death. No matter how much people rationally tried to explain why it wasn't my fault I wouldn't believe them. I'd convinced myself that it was, and I can be hard-headed. Surely there must've been a way for me to save him. Then there was the fact that Mike was dead and I wasn't. 'Why's that?' I agonized. It's called survivor's guilt. Guilt upon guilt squashed me down. To numb the pain that I was feeling, I drank, and not just that one night with Jake. When I was idle my mind would keep bringing me back to that fateful day of the canoe trip, the futile cry for help in Mike's eyes. Then there'd be the Grim Reaper reminding me of my promise and whose fault it was. He haunted my dreams at night. Occasionally he'd rear his ugly head during the day when I'd least expect it. And so, I kept drinking. Free time became my enemy.

During that winter break Jake and I went to Sun Valley, Idaho, to do some skiing. Chelsea and her friend joined us. We rented a condo at the resort and had a great time. This place was a winter wonderland. Chelsea's friend didn't mind spending time with Jake, helping him improve his skiing. Meanwhile, Chelsea and I schussed all over the rest of the mountain. She was an excellent skier, but I found out her favorite thing came afterwards. That was hanging out in the lodge drinking pina coladas while being warmed by the burning logs in the fireplace. We'd snuggle and drink our way into oblivion. I really enjoyed my time with her. The only thing that concerned me about Chelsea was the little red pills.

That Spring I went back to school and immersed myself in my studies. In three years I planned on having a degree in business administration with an emphasis in marketing. I also got my old job back at the convenience store where I worked before my trip. The manager there loved my work ethic. He was true to his word letting someone else go to make room for me when I returned. I never drank at school or work, that came afterwards. I was becoming a functional alcoholic.

My mom saw what was happening and kept urging me to see a psychologist. I balked. I knew I could handle it myself. Dad didn't raise a wimp. Mom said she could drive me. I told her I could drive myself if I wanted. She said she'd pay. I said why waste the money. Then she remembered it was covered by insurance, totally. She said, I said. The faucet kept dripping. It was making me go berserk. Finally, I gave in, but only to get my mom off my back.

After introductions, and telling my female therapist about the trip and its fatal ending, the visit went something like this:

"How does that make you feel?" she asked.

"How does what make me feel?"

"Your cousin dying."

"It makes me feel like crap," I answered. "He was my best friend. How would it make you feel if your best friend were killed?"

"I wouldn't feel very good either," she responded.

"Exactly. Wouldn't you feel guilty if the thing that killed your friend was your idea and you'd promised to take care of them?"

"Maybe it was an unrealistic promise."

"Nevertheless, if you believed it, even though said partly in jest, wouldn't you feel guilty?"

"Well, I guess so."

"Exactly. It's a normal reaction. I'll get over it," I said confidently.

"Your mom thinks you may be developing a drinking problem because of all this."

"Do you drink?" I asked.

"Well, yes."

"I imagine this job can get stressful, working on other people's problems all the time?"

"It can be."

"Does a drink help you unwind after a hard day?"

"Well, yes."

"Sounds to me like you may be developing a drinking problem."

"I'm not."

"Are you sure you're not in denial?"

"Hold on," my therapist said, seeming a bit flustered. "I ask the questions here."

My appointment lasted a whopping hour and a half. By the time I got out of there I'll bet the shrink needed a session on her own couch. When she got home that night I also wouldn't be surprised if she had a double of whatever she was drinking. Truth is, I could have used some help in dealing with Mike's death. I was too blind to see it or too proud to admit it. The drinking, well, I discounted that with the notion I could quit whenever I wanted.

The next two years were jam-packed. I took a full load of classes, worked full time at the convenience store, and was in a full-fledged steamy relationship with Chelsea. I managed to keep good grades at school. At work I got moved into the corporate offices. and Chelsea, well, let's just say I was her main squeeze. She'd travel out to San Diego to see me and I'd travel back to Boise to see her. She was a looker, something to behold, but what attracted me most to her was her vivaciousness. She always seemed to be bubbling over with energy. In our conversations I found out that the reason her family moved during high school was because of her father's work. She also told me about the red pills. They were a prescription for a woman's problem, a hormonal, time-of-the-month issue. Nothing to get alarmed about there.

It was February 1977. I'd just started my senior year, with plans to graduate in the Fall, when I got a call. It was Chelsea. Normally it'd be no big deal, we talked a lot, but…

"Hi Mark," she beamed, like this was the highmark of her life.

"Hi Chelski. Miss you."

"Mark, I've got some wonderful news for you," she gushed through the phone.

"Chelsea, you been drinking?"

"No, you nut. It's not even noon yet. Guess."

"You got an A on your accounting test."

"No, that's not it. Guess again."

"You got an F on your accounting test," I kidded.

"No, you nut. I got a B, but that's not it either. This is the most exciting day of my life."

"Okay, I give up. What is it?"

"Are you sitting down?"

"I'm sitting."

"Are you sure you're sitting?" Chelsea again warned excitedly. I was beginning to wonder if she was high on some drug.

"I'm sitting already. Let's hear this wonderful news."

"I'm pregnant," she screamed with delight, like her team had just won the World Series.

I was in shock. There's no way. I thought we'd been so careful. Maybe there was some other guy in her life. My head started swimming in circles. I felt like a fish floundering on an out-of-control carousel. I was speechless. There was an awkward silence.

"Honey, did you hear me? I'm pregnant. We're going to have a baby."

"You're not fooling with me, are you?" I knew she was serious, but I felt like I needed to ask on the outside chance she was messin' with me. This was huge.

"No fooling. You're going to be a father," she said like I'd be overjoyed. She definitely was.

"But I thought you said we were protected. You didn't miss taking your birth control pills did you?" I questioned.

"No, I took them faithfully. It's fate. We're meant to be together, to have a baby."

"It's not that simple Chelsea. We're still in school. We're not even married."

"Are you upset?" Chelsea's mood changed. "You don't sound very happy. You're not thinking I should get an abortion, are you?"

"No, no, no way! I don't want you to get an abortion. I don't believe in them. And I'm not upset. Surprised, but not upset. I just never anticipated this."

"Honey, are you sure you're not upset?"

"No, I mean yes. What I mean is, I'm not upset. It's just now sinking in. How cool is this, we're having a baby!" I exclaimed with as much enthusiasm as I could muster up. "Have you told your parents?"

"Not yet. I wanted you to be the first to know."

"Why don't you tell them and I'll tell mine. I've got to get to work right now. I'll call you later and we can start making plans."

"Okay."

"Chelski." I paused.

"Yes."

"Congratulations, mommy."

I could feel her smile radiating over the phone.

Truthfully, though, I was upset. I simply didn't have the heart to rain on Chelsea's parade. I didn't want to spoil her joyous moment. But we still had school to finish and careers to work on. There goes any free time that was left. A baby was really going to put a crimp on things. And what was this "honey" stuff. She'd never called me that before. It sounded like a married couple, like it was laced with expectation. A friend once told me; if you play, eventually you'll have to pay. Well, the volcano has erupted. The lava's flown and the ash has been spewed. What now would the landscape of my life become? Desolate like some of the land Mike and I had ridden through or lush like a tropical island? I was hoping for the later. To fortify my choice I bought a bottle of wine.

Chapter Ten

Un-Real-ing Life

To marry Chelsea or not to marry Chelsea was the question I now faced. Her father was going to make sure I did. At least that's the impression I got from him. Two months later we did get married in Las Vegas. It had the appearance of being a shotgun wedding. However, I married Chelsea because I thought it was the right thing to do. After the wedding I didn't like being around my father-in-law. He made me extremely nervous. There were times when I wondered if I'd get out of his presence alive. I used to think he liked me, but now I wasn't so sure. I saw a whole new side of him, one filled with intense anger bordering on rage. I know Chelsea and I screwed up, getting pregnant and all, but it seemed like there was something deeper, almost dark going on. I also got the feeling that he was glad to be rid of her. His wife on the other hand was the polar opposite, always kind and considerate to me.

Chelsea dropped out of school and moved to San Diego. Financially I was living a charmed life so we were able to buy a house. Why rent and make somebody else rich I thought. I was working. The money I won in Reno with Mike I had invested in gold futures and it paid off. The price of gold had climbed while stocks had been dropping. Then there was our quick inexpensive wedding in Vegas. It had me feeling like I had an extra thousand dollars to play with. So while we were there, I played and the casino paid. I ended up walking away with sixteen thousand dollars, enough for the down payment on the house.

We bought a three bedroom, two bath ranch-style house with a two-car garage and a swimming pool. It cost us a small fortune, fifty-two thousand dollars. Mom loved it because it was in a nice neighborhood not far from hers. She was looking forward to spending lots of time with her first grandchild.

Chelsea didn't have to work. That turned out to be a blessing because she was having a rough pregnancy and was able to stay at home. She was constantly complaining of nausea and pain. I got yelled at a lot. I'd bring her some flowers, a card, or a box of chocolates and she'd be nice, for awhile, then she'd start snapping at me some more. Sometimes it would be for a petty thing and sometimes there was no rhyme or reason to it at all. Then a horrid thought struck me, what if she was like this normally? I found myself studying more at school and working longer hours to avoid the annoyance. I'm not a conflict type guy. I'm more of a 'what the world needs now is love' type guy. Hmm, sounds like another song. Donovan's Irish Pub became a popular hangout of mine.

One day, around Chelsea's seventh month, I decided to surprise her and a couple of her old high school friends she'd reconnected with. She'd invited them to our home. It was lunchtime. I rarely made it home for lunch. I bought a half-gallon of rocky-road ice cream and a jar of creamy peanut butter, two of my wife's cravings. 'Oh, will they ever be surprised,' I thought.

"Surprise!" I hollered as I opened the door.

Three pairs of eyes looked up at me from around the coffee table. There was some white powder on it, some straws, a bottle of wine, and some glasses.

"Hi, honey," Chelsea smiled sheepishly.

"What the hell is going on here?" I asked my wife irately.

"We're having a little eency weency party to make me feel better. And I feel wonderful!"

"Out! OUT!" I yelled, enraged by what I saw. "You two, leave. NOW!"

"Honey, that's no way to treat my friends. This is Betsy, and this is Francisca."

"Hi, I'm Betsy," one of them said. "I made the American flag."

"Did not," the other responded. "You'd be way old and your face would look like a prune."

"Did too. It was for a play I was in in sixth grade." The three of them giggled.

"Are you all crazy?" I said in disbelief.

"Honey …"

"Don't honey me. Betsy and Francisca, you need to leave, and quickly before I lose my patience."

"Chill, Mark," Betsy said. "Everything's cool. We're leaving. You know, you should try some of this stuff. It'll help you relax."

"Out of my house," I ordered angrily as I backhanded the pile of white powder sending it up in a cloud of dust.

"Hey, what you…"

"OUT!"

As the two of them left, I overheard them telling each other how unlucky Chelsea was marrying such an uptight guy. I should have called the police on them, but then there was my wife. What would happen with her? I had a drink to calm myself down. Chelsea was in no condition to hold a rational conversation. She was wasted. How was this cocaine episode going to affect our baby? Come to think of it, how long had this been goin' on? She'd been seeing these friends for months. It was beginning to sound like another gone bad love song, only in this one the other lover is a drug. I took the rest of the day off and scheduled an appointment for the next day to consult with her obstetrician.

"How long have you been using coke?" the doctor asked.

"Most of my life."

"Most of your life?" a startled doctor responded.

"Yes, my family drinks a lot of it. My dad buys it by the case." Chelsea grinned.

"Chelsea, answer the doctor," I said firmly. "This is no joking matter." I could feel my blood pressure rising.

"Okay already. It's no big deal. That was the first and only time I've ever used it."

"Why would you do such a thing?" I asked anxiously. "You know you're pregnant. You're carrying our baby."

"I'm sorry. I was bored and feeling like a blimp. It's depressing."

"Doctor," I questioned, "how is this going to affect the baby? And please don't sugar-coat it. I really want to know what we are in for."

"Most likely it won't," he answered. "Adverse effects usually only occur with continued use or addiction."

I breathed a sigh of relief.

He continued, "Are you using any other drugs?"

"Absolutely not!" she replied defensively.

"What about your prescription?" I asked.

"What prescription?"

"You know, the little red pills," I reminded.

"Oh, those. It's no big deal."

"What are you taking?" the doctor wanted to know. "It's important to know. It can have an effect on both you and the baby."

"Chelsea, what the heck is going on here?" I asked in angst.

Chelsea's face flushed red. An extreme paranoia set in. "You can't make me stop taking them. I'll die. I need them to survive. Please don't make me stop," she pleaded.

Long story short, my wife was hooked on amphetamines. She was 'speed'ing her way through life. She had outright lied to me about the pills. Turns out she had lied about her cocaine use too. Yesterday was no way near her first time. The doctor warned us that our baby could be born prematurely. That it would probably have a low birth weight. He also told us that it could be born with some mental retardation, cerebral palsy, or possibly have some auditory or visual problems. I wanted to tell the doctor to stop, this was more than my heart could bear, but I needed to know what we were facing. He further warned us that our baby was likely to be less responsive and have a harder time bonding with mom. That would make for more emotional difficulties down the road. Finally, he mentioned being born addicted. There'd be withdrawals. He'd heard of babies having shrill cries, agitation, even jerking.

I was mortified! I was furious with my wife. I was even more furious with myself. How could I have allowed something like this to happen? How could I have not seen what was going on? When we got home I went through the whole house with a fine tooth comb looking for drugs. To my wife's chagrin, what I found went swirling down the toilet. There were going to be a lot of high sewer rats the next few days. Then I enrolled Chelsea in an outpatient rehab program. She definitely needed some help. And me, I needed to talk to somebody. I also needed some fortitude. Where should I go?

Well, I thought about going to my mom's. She was always understanding and offered compassionate advice. But I didn't want to upset her, especially over the baby. This was going to be her first grandchild and she was so excited. I thought about going to my church, but that would be awkward. I hadn't been there in such a long time. What, do I only go to church now when I need help? And what would I say about having to get married or about my wife's drug problem? I'd made a mess of my life. How's that going to make me look? My pride and image control shot that choice down. Truth is, I think I knew where I was going to go from the start, my favorite watering hole, Donovan's.

"I'll have my usual," I said to Bob as I pulled a stool up to the bar.

"What's up?" he asked. "You seem bothered by something tonight."

"Bob, you are so perceptive."

"You're one of my favorite customers. You get to know a person over time. I bet it's your wife again, isn't it?"

"Yeah."

"You know, you should get her into some anger management therapy," he suggested.

"It's more than that now, although she was very upset when I flushed her drugs down the toilet."

"Drugs? I thought she was pregnant," Bob wondered outloud.

"She is. And today I found out she's addicted to speed and has been snorting cocaine for some time."

"Hey, buddy," drawled the guy on the next stool over, "sounds like my ex-wife."

"What did you do about it?" I asked.

"Didn't you hear me? I said Ex. Drugs spell a heap o' trouble. With us it got worser and worser."

"I'm not going to divorce her. I made a vow. For better or for worse, 'til death do us part."

"Then one of ya will have'ta die."

"Enough," Bob said, stepping in.

"Okay, Mr. Bartender. Get my buddy here another of whatever he's drinking. It's on me. He's gonna need it."

I spent a couple hours there. It felt good to talk, to share some of my struggles. I left somewhat anesthetized and feeling much better. I was hoping for peace when I got home, but I knew the chances for that were slim to none. Chelsea had her anger issues and when the clock struck nine it usually seemed to ratchet up a couple notches. I called it 'the witching hour'. It was only a short drive home, less than two miles. That was a good thing because I'd have less time to think about things by myself. I needed distractions to keep from stewing. No sooner had I gotten on the road when I looked in my rear-view mirror only to see flashing lights.

'Oh crap,' I thought, and quickly popped in a breath mint as I pulled over. The policeman approached my window. I rolled it down.

"Can I see your driver's license?" he asked.

"Yes, sir," I responded politely and handed it to him.

"Where are you headed?"

"Home," I answered. "It's only a mile from here."

"Where you coming from?"

"From Donovan's."

"How much have you had to drink?"

"I just had a quick one to help me sleep tonight." I crossed my toes.

"Just one?"

"Yes, sir."

"The reason I pulled you over is because you have a right rear taillight out," he informed. "I'm going to give you a fix-it ticket."

"Thank you, officer, I didn't realize it. I'll get it fixed right away. Don't want to be driving without a taillight. That can be dangerous."

"Drive safely," he admonished.

"Yes sir, I will."

He drove off. Phew! Was I ever relieved.

The following day I became a private investigator. I had come to realize the hard way that I didn't really know my wife. I guess it was her pretty face, the pretty skirts showing off her gorgeous legs, and her spontaneity that had me mesmerized, blinded. Hormones had won out over brains. Not smart. The resulting pregnancy forced the marriage in a way. I sure didn't want my child calling somebody else daddy. During this time, a buried, more intense anger reared its head from an unknown grave deep inside Chelsea. That anger kept escalating. There were near constant nightly battles. Anything I said sparked an argument. I was never right, always wrong. And now came this new drug revelation. Fireworks exploded! Donovan's was no longer just a watering hole, it had become my sanctuary, my refuge from the storm. I could think there. I thought over and over again about all that was happening and came to a decision — I can help my wife. I can fix her. In order to do that, though, I was going to need to know where she was coming from, what made her this way.

I contacted as many of Chelsea's family and friends as I could. What I pieced together I found rather startling. First off, she'd lied to me again. She was quite good at it. How was I ever going to be able to trust her? Turns out her parents had moved their family to Boise to get Chelsea away from a drug culture she'd gotten entangled in. She'd been in and out of recovery programs for years. That's probably why I never really got to know her in high school. We hung out in totally different crowds, and it was a large school, over four thousand kids. I was told her father was sick of dealing with it. Perhaps that's why he seemed so glad to be rid of her. Let someone else have to cope with her drug problems. But why now the rage from him?

That's what the second thing I uncovered dealt with, or so I surmised. I found out Chelsea's dad was a full-blown alcoholic. It was the family secret. He'd lost a number of jobs because of it. He had a low self esteem. To make himself look bigger in his own eyes he was constantly berating his wife and two daughters. It made him feel powerful. He was a mean drunk too. I was told that oftentimes he'd come home hammered and thrash out at his family. They were barraged with verbal abuse. Sometimes it had even turned physical with one of them getting smacked or thrown up against a wall. Mom became the enabler, always making excuses for dad. Two people I talked with were convinced that Chelsea was sexually assaulted by her father on more than one occasion. I got to thinking about that. Maybe that explained his rage. I know it sounds weird, but what if Chelsea's dad had come to think of her more as another wife than a daughter. Then she gets pregnant by me and I in essence steal her away from him. His love turns into a twisted jealous hate. Who knows what lurks in someone else's mind?

Another thought came to me, 'What if the baby... no, let's not get too imaginative lest I drive myself nuts.'

The last big thing I dug up did have to do with Chelsea's pregnancy. I found out through her sister that she tried to get pregnant. She stopped taking her birth control pills in hopes that she would. Her scheme, her deception, worked. She got pregnant and I married her. She wagered most assuredly that I would and I did. It was her ticket out of a bad situation. That raised another question in my head. Did Chelsea really love me, or was I merely an escape? Was I being conned, lied to again? My ego didn't want to take that hit so I chose to believe that indeed she did love me. That sure, I was used as an escape, but more in the sense of being her rescuer, like a knight in shining armor. I'd come to save my princess who was being held captive in a castle dungeon. With that mindset, I thought I could handle this ordeal. I'd already rescued Chelsea from her father, now I could rescue her from herself. Or could I?

Our baby was born premature by about a month. He was lightweight and on the lethargic side. I kept thinking, 'Oh, my God! What have I done to my son?' The doctor seemed to think that things would normalize over time. But what if, what if they didn't, I worried? ***What-ifs*** can really mess with your mind. I felt responsible. I felt horribly guilty. And so I continued to self-medicate at Donovan's.

We named him Mark. I was Mark Jr., named after my dad. My son, in that same tradition, now was the III. I was hoping that he'd be as proud of me and carrying that name as I was of it and my dad.

When we got home from the hospital nothing changed with Chelsea. My hope that Chelsea's behavior was simply the product of pregnancy got shot down. You'd think she would be happy being a new mommy, but that wasn't the case here. She still blew up in fits of anger. In fact, I think it got worse. It was like floodwaters breaching a dam. And just as the doctor feared might happen, mommy and Mark III were not bonding very well. I connected with our baby more than Chelsea did. The rejection she already was feeling got heavier. It made her even angrier. I, her outlet, was showered with more tongue lashings. A few times she even took a swing at me. Sound familiar? I'd have spent more time at the pub but I worried about my son's safety.

All during this time I kept up a torrid pace. I completed my schooling at San Diego State, graduating magna com laude with a degree in business. At work I continued to thrive. My goal was to shoot up the corporate ladder. I visualized it, could see it happening. With school now behind me, I had even more time to invest in my career. I worked long hours. I buried myself in my work and justified it with the notion that I was providing for my family. There was a mortgage to pay, gas and lights, food, diapers, it all added up. On top of that was the cost of Chelsea's therapy to deal with her addiction. And then there was the nanny I hired part-time to help with little Mark. I enjoyed working a lot, but being at work was also a form of conflict management for me. It's called avoidance.

In March of 1978 I got a call at work. It was Chelsea.

"Hi, honey," she began. It sounded too sweet. I knew something was going on.

"Yes, dear, what's up?"

"Honey, I've decided I'm through with drugs, once and for all."

"Okay… that would be nice," I responded with a large measure of cautious skepticism. I'd heard that line before. "What brings this on?"

"The rabbit died."

"The rabbit died. What rabbit? You didn't get Mark a pet, did you?"

"No. Don't you get it? The rabbit died." she repeated.

"Come on, Chelsea, I'm at work. I really don't get it. Do I need to keep guessing?"

"No, silly, I'm pregnant!" she exclaimed. "We're going to have another baby."

Chelsea indeed was pregnant again. Before this latest revelation, I was getting a lot of unsolicited counsel from people at work and at the pub. Most of them knew the situation with Chelsea and the struggles we faced and they all seemed to think it would never change. The drugs, the abuse, and the anger were going to be enormously hard things for Chelsea to give up. The advice I was getting was to leave her or face a lifetime of misery. It made me think. But here she was, again pregnant. I didn't feel like I could bail out now. What about my kids? How would they do? Maybe another child would help straighten her out, I hoped. So I hung in there.

In November of that year, we had another boy and named him Mike, after my cousin. Chelsea did manage to stay drug-free for a few months in the beginning of her pregnancy. Unfortunately, the lure of drugs won out over her willpower and she buckled in on numerous occasions. Like his brother, Mike, too, was born underweight. This heaped on another bucket-load of guilt. Was this my fault? This time I'd been warned. I hadn't heeded the advice of many who kept telling me to divorce Chelsea. Take your boy with you and leave they'd said. She is a bad influence on him. She's a danger. I had the divorce "gun" in my hand, but I just couldn't pull the trigger. Deep down inside I loved her. Occasionally she'd have a few good days in a row. I'd even go so far as to say she'd be happy and we'd do something fun. It gave me a glimmer of optimism. And so I kept thinking, hoping, that things would get better, permanently.

Growing up I always imagined that I'd find the right lady, settle down, and then the rest of my life would be marital bliss. Boy, was I wrong. The first couple of years were definitely not what I'd hoped for or expected. 'What had I done to myself?' I questioned. Nothing had improved. The next ten years I trudged through a marital abyss. Chelsea was in and out of rehab programs. At one point she struggled with anorexia and became a skeleton of the beauty I'd married. After working through that, bulimia became her captor. It tortured me to watch her destroy herself. She changed from one psychologist to another to yet another trying to find one that would tell her what her tickling ears wanted to hear, not the truth. Some obliged, and I wondered if Chelsea wasn't merely an income stream for them. Sometimes I also wondered if Chelsea even cared about how she was disrupting the family, if she really wanted to get better. She appeared content with the way she acted.

Perhaps it was her comfort zone, what she got used to when growing up. Maybe to change simply didn't feel right to her. Whatever it was, it was driving me crazy. One thing I did know. Through it all she sure seemed to relish the attention.

My boys were the glue that helped hold my marriage together. My, my, my. My boys, my marriage. What happened to the word "our"? Well, it didn't seem like Chelsea wanted any ownership in the boys. They were a constant source of irritation to her. As for our marriage, it seemed like there was no give on her part. She only wanted a sugar daddy, someone to take care of her, give her whatever she desired. So why were the boys the glue? Somewhere I had read an article by a noted psychologist that really stuck with me. It said that divorce is especially hard on children. It said that children usually fare better in a two parent, mom and dad type home, even if the parents don't get along. I didn't want to heap any more hardship on little Mark and Mike. They had enough challenges right out of the chute.

In 1982 I got wooed away from the company I worked for. Another company offered me a large salary increase, the chance to move up the corporate ladder quicker, and a new company car of my choice. There was no way I was going to pass up an opportunity like that. The one downside was that it involved travel. This meant less time to spend with the boys. There'd be less time to read or show flashcards to them to improve their mental acuity, and less time to work with their physical coordination skills. Both were lacking. The guilt I felt intensified.

My boys were held back a year in school. Even so, they still struggled greatly. This was foreign to me. School and athletics always came easy. I had hoped my boys would be chips off the old block, like father, like sons. Looking at them was hard sometimes. I knew who was responsible for this. I hired a tutor to help them. They rebelled. Many times, when I got home from work or a business trip, I'd be met with a frantic message from one of their teachers. They both had developed behavioral problems. Chelsea couldn't cope with it. That put it all on me. I'll tell you, life away from work was tough. My sports, a little skiing, tennis, and racquetball, helped relieve the stress, but that wasn't enough.

In the middle of those years I got my first DUI. It infuriated me to no end. I was nice to the arresting officer and the judge, but inside I was fuming. They had no idea what I had to deal with on a daily basis. I had to drink to maintain my sanity. It was my wife's fault. The thousands of dollars it cost irked me even more. There were the fines, the attorney's fees, the increased insurance costs, etc., etc. I worked hard for that money. It was like flushing hundred dollar bills down the toilet. What a waste. They certainly weren't going to be of any use to those high sewer rats.

In 1988 I got my second DUI. The judge handling my case ordered me to go listen to a victim of a drunk driver tell their story. That person belonged to an organization called MADD (Mothers Against Drunk Driving). 'Oh great!' I thought. 'Now I've got to listen to some screaming mother with an axe to grind against anyone who likes to drink a little.' I went to hear this person begrudgingly. Afterall, I drive safely. I'd never been in an accident. I knew my limits. And besides, the bar I frequent is less than two miles from my house, that's just a hop, skip, and a jump away. I should never have been arrested. I was almost home.

When I arrived at the classroom there were a dozen others already waiting. I made it thirteen, a baker's dozen. I knew that when the lady speaker showed up we'd all be scorched in her oven of wrath. What a waste of time. It was a joke. Nobody here had hurt anyone. Only a couple of people here really looked like they needed help, but as for the rest of us, huh. I'll bet the police had simply used us to fill some ticket quota. Then the guest speaker appeared. Surprise, surprise! I was expecting a mother, our speaker was a father. A he, not a she. That seemed like false advertising to me. I really did not want to be there.

"Good evening," our speaker began. "My name is Bart. And as you can see, I am not a mother."

"Yeah, what's up with that?" asked one of the two guys who I thought needed help. He looked like he was high on something.

"That's a good question," Bart responded tactfully.

'Oh, this guy is good,' I thought. 'Did you see the way he handled this belligerent idiot's question. He must be in sales.'

Bart went on, "Mothers Against Drunk Driving was started in 1980 by a mother who lost her teenage daughter to a drunk driver. Since then many have rallied to her cause. You don't need to be a mother to belong. There are men and women, married and single in our organization. People of all colors, creeds, and income levels have joined. They are all united with the same mission, to eliminate drunk driving and the senseless deaths it causes."

"I don't get it. Why the big fuss?" asked the other questionable person in the room. It definitely gave away his shoe-size IQ.

"Can anyone here answer that?" the speaker asked.

"Deaths," I quickly answered in exasperation. 'Wasn't this guy listening.' "The big deal is that some people are getting killed." 'No more stupid questions,' I thought. 'They're slowing down the meeting. I want out of here.'

"That was another good question and answer," Bart affirmed. "In fact, last year nearly 20,000 people were killed in drunk driving crashes. That's almost half the number of soldiers we lost in combat in all thirteen years of the Vietnam War. And these deaths are totally preventable. It all comes down to a choice — not to drink and drive. Does anyone here know how far a car doing 65mph travels in one second?"

Nobody raised their hand.

Bart answered his own question. "About ninety feet, a long way. In a quarter of a second, not much more than the blink of an eye, it's about twenty-two feet. That's why, as you can see, you don't want your reaction time compromised when driving. Does anybody know what alcohol is?"

The idiot's hand shot up. "Something I like to drink," he blurted out with a pleased grin on his face like he'd just solved some big mystery of life. I'm thinking, this guy must have small feet too.

Again Bart responded graciously. "In the right situation alcoholic beverages can be enjoyed. When you combine drinking with driving though, it's dangerous. Alcohol is a depressant. It slows down your reaction time. It doesn't take a rocket scientist to figure out why alcohol is involved in nearly forty percent of all traffic deaths. Three out of every ten people will be involved in an alcohol-related crash sometime during their lifetime. I pray that none of you will ever have to experience what I did four years ago. It is still my living nightmare!"

Bart went on with a few more statistics and then told us his story. It had been a warm summer night. Bart was coming home late from work. When he got to his street it was blocked off with yellow cones and emergency vehicles. He parked his car and quickly went to investigate. Revolving lights lit up a small horde of onlookers and then he saw two orange body bags lying on the ground. Bart had a gut-wrenching feeling and began running towards them. He was intercepted by a police officer. The officer told him there was nothing to see, nothing he could do. Bart knew. He went into shock.

As it turned out, his worst nightmare was realized. They were his two teenage boys. They were best friends, only twenty months apart in age. They had been on their way to a nearby drugstore to get a couple of sodas when a drunk driver mowed them down. It turned out to be their next-door neighbor. He was a nice enough fellow. Unfortunately, he had a penchant for drinking which he usually did at a pub only a couple miles away from his home. He wound up in prison. Bart's wife couldn't handle the grief and committed suicide six months later. Bart lives in a mental prison himself. It's called the prison of his mind. He speaks as a way of coping, of trying to make good out of his tragic circumstance.

By the time Bart was finished speaking I was in tears. How sad. How preventable. Losing two boys, dang, they could have been mine. And their neighbor, that very well could've been me. I thanked Bart for sharing and gave him an empathetic hug. As I left I promised myself, and him, that I'd never drink and drive again.

Over the next month I became aware of something that really rattled me. I seemed to always be asking for a ride or taking a taxi. 'If that's the case,' I thought, and indeed it was, I realized that, 'I must have a drinking problem. Could I be an alcoholic?' I resolved to check myself into an intensive two week live-in rehab program. Just as soon as I got back from an important upcoming business trip.

"You're a failure," a voice said.

"Who said that?" I queried as I opened my eyes and looked around the living room. Nobody was there. It had been a long day at the office. After a few drinks at Donovan's on my way home from work, I simply wanted to relax in my recliner and listen to some music from one of my favorite artists, Cat Stevens. Staying true to my word, I'd taken a taxi home. In the morning, I was going to jog back to the pub to retrieve my car. A little exercise couldn't hurt. Sitting there, I must've dozed off and been dreaming. I closed my eyes and drifted back asleep.

"You're a failure," the voice said again, only louder.

This time I recognized it, opened my eyes, and saw him staring at me from a picture on the wall. "I thought I got rid of you for good," I cursed. My Grim Reaper taunter was back.

"You can't get rid of me. I'll always be with you. Ha ha ha," he laughed devilishly. "Ha ha ha ha."

I grabbed the remote and threw it at the picture knocking it off the wall. He was still there harassing me.

"You're a failure," he scoffed. "You couldn't save your best friend. You can't fix your wife. Your marriage is trashed, and, ha ha ha, look at your boys. Failure with a capital F. You're the man of the house. You're in charge. It's all on you. Ha ha ha ha."

"AAGH! Leave me alone," I uttered as I lurched from my chair and headed to the kitchen for some help. He followed me with his verbal assault. A couple of tall ones later and that voice was silenced. Why was he back in my life after all these years? Why?

Three days later I flew to Denver on business.

Chapter Eleven

Temptation, and a Repulse Impulse

The Board loved my new promotional ideas for our fast-food take-out chain of restaurants. Our company, ODD, which stands for Our Deli Delivers, had grown from 200 to over 400 outlets. This all happened on my watch, since my inception as VP in charge of product development and promotion. My new position had come only five years earlier when the CEO took a liking to me after my suggested name change and the company's subsequent meteoric rise. It had been failing miserably. Bankruptcy had loomed. But now it was the darling of Wall Street. As an ODD man I was even asked to appear on a couple of late-night talk shows. My business life was booming.

I left the board meeting pumped! My hard work was paying off and I felt so appreciated. This called for a celebration. On cloud nine I took the elevator and floated down to the bar. When I exited the elevator there was Teresa using one of the two pay- phones on the wall outside the cocktail lounge. She too was on the Board and was an avid supporter of my ideas. She looked over at me and smiled as I deposited my dime in the slot to call my wife. The operator answered.

"This is the operator. How can I help you?"

"I'd like to place a collect call to my home in San Diego," I responded and gave her the number. Chelsea answered.

"Will you accept the charges?" the operator asked.

"Hell, no," she blurted out loudly. "You tell him not to come home. No, wait, I accept. Let me talk to the son of a ****," she continued with slurred speech.

"Hi, dear. How are …"

"How come you didn't call earlier?" came her irate response.

"Dear, I tried but ..."

"Like hell you tried. And stop calling me dear. What do you think I am, an animal?"

I hesitated.

"You think I'm an animal. Don't you?"

"No, honey, I …"

"Now you're arguing with me. Why do you always argue with me? And what's this honey stuff? You think I'm a bee, huh? You think I'm going to sting you?"

"I love you."

"Don't patronize me. You know I hate being home alone. I've got all the doors and windows locked and I hear noises outside."

"I'm catching a flight home tomorrow. By the way, how are the boys?"

"That's it. All you care about is the boys. You're a horrible husband. I hate you! I wish you were dead!!!" CLICK!

'I love you too,' I thought as I stood there stunned. One minute I'm feeling on top of the world, the next, like I'm rotting in a box buried six feet underground. Nothing new. It'd been like this since shortly after we were married. A 'why I was in this mess' tape replayed in my head for the umpteenth time. I needed to re-rationalize my reasoning.

I hadn't known Chelsea had a drug problem before we were married. And once I found out, I figured I could help her. I was strong enough to handle it, to fix her. Hey, I was able to cope with my father, whom I was very close to, dying. So what if he was buried on my seventeenth birthday. And I was able to cope with my best friend dying only two years later. Hey, I was mentally tough. Could I have been wrong? So what if I drank a little to fortify myself and assuage some of my feelings. I'm only human. What could one expect? I wasn't hurting anyone. And besides, I was going to work on that when I returned to San Diego.

Teresa overheard most of my conversation. During the last few years she'd become more than just a business associate. She'd become a loyal friend, a confidant. I'd shared some of my struggles with her. She seemed to understand the loneliness I felt, having a wife whose life was pretty much consumed with drugs, abuse issues, and anger. As much as I liked Teresa, my relationship with her had stayed strictly platonic.

"Do you mind if I join you for a drink?" Teresa asked sympathetically.

"No, I'd like that," I replied.

We headed into the uncrowded lounge and found a booth in the corner. A lady blues singer was singing a sultry song about love gone wrong. A cocktail waitress lit the candle on our table and took our order, two pina coladas. The flickering candlelight danced in Teresa's big brown eyes. She was so nice. And she was well-endowed too. Her low-cut blouse made it difficult for me to maintain eye contact. She was a looker. And, have I mentioned, she was so nice. We talked about the days' successes, and a couple drinks later, about my phone conversation.

"Mark, I hate to see you down. You deserve better than this," Teresa empathized.

"I'll be all right. I've learned to deal with it."

"Deal with it? You shouldn't have to spend the rest of your life dealing with it. The drugs, the alcohol, the anger, the bitterness. I'm telling you, you deserve better than this. You deserve to be happy."

"So what are you saying?"

Teresa scooted closer to me and grabbed my hand. Then came her proposition, "Come spend the night with me. Let's enjoy life, each other."

'Whoa, where'd this come from?' I thought. I'd be lying if I said I hadn't thought about her several times before, but I was always able to dismiss the possibility. She was so enticing, her hand so warm. My heart sped up. I wanted to, but I was married.

"Teresa, I can't. I'm married. I made a vow, for better or for worse." I emphasized the worse part.

She held my hand up to her lips and gently kissed it. I could feel my resolve weakening. "How much worse does it have to get?" she asked. "You're an honorable man, the kind of man I've dreamed of spending my whole life with."

"I don't know." This sure wasn't sounding like a one-time fling thing.

"Come on," she urged. "Chelsea doesn't appreciate you one bit. I would never take you for granted. I truly believe I could make you happy for the rest of your life. At least let me try."

Her perfume was fogging up my brain, maybe the drinks too. "Okay," I surrendered. Heck, I did deserve better. "I'll meet you at your hotel in an hour. I'm just gonna have one more drink, grab some clothes, and I'm on my way."

"You can let yourself in," Teresa said as she handed me a key to her room. "I'll be waiting."

The hotel she was staying at was only a couple miles down the road from there. I ordered another drink. This called for a double. While drinking it I kept rationalizing why this was okay. I did deserve better than the way I was being treated. All Chelsea really cared about was herself. I doubt any man in my situation would have turned Teresa down. She genuinely cares about my life. Chelsea sure doesn't. She's more like a cranky embittered roommate than a wife. Heck, when I am home she usually doesn't like me anyway. If she's not beating up on me she often treats me like I'm not there, like I don't exist. I got out a pen and paper and began writing. I felt like expressing myself.

I loved you.

Three drinks, three tears, I think of years gone by me.
I'm up, I'm down, spinnin' 'round my mind goes.
I love you, I don't, I would, I could,
Does it matter?
Spending time with you and buying what?
Half-filled minutes,
Hours without days,
An emptiness, a loneliness, feeling stray.
I spent my time with you, babe,
Yes I spent my time with you,

Oh I spent my time with you, babe,
And bought the blues.

Four drinks, four tears, more years.
I think I've got you, then I don't.
I drift, then float, and when you're near,
Your warmth, I feel, ...will burn me.
Searing flesh, eyes seem so true, yet hiding you.
What can I do?
My hopes and dreams become a fantasy,
An unreality, but,
They carry me through the night,
And make my day seem true, not blue.

Five drinks, more tears, more leers, more jeers.
The crowd laughs,
At me,
At you,
The silly, not so silly things we do.
We, am I to say, you and me,
Are we?

Six, seven drinks, stream tears.
All the years gone by.
I lied, to me, to you. Reality too true.
Too drunk, too drunk to care.
Dare I say what's on my mind? Has drink released
the bind? To say what's on my mind,
...what's on my mind, ... what's on my mind.
I love you.
I really love you. I love you more than you could
know, yet in my doubts, my fears, more tears,
I go,
Too scared to know if you loved me.

I love you. I love you, I loved you.

Eight drinks, dry tears, endless years
On cosmic plains, no more pains,
It's through.
Too bad for me, too bad for you.

It seemed so sad, what I'd written. Was this a death ode to my marriage? I went on rationalizing. If we did split up I'm sure she would be happier, probably much happier. All I seem to bring her is grief. I'm sure I can make Teresa happy. And she's so nice. And …and the more I thought about it, the more convinced I became. My feelings, my desire for Teresa, grew. I downed the rest of my drink and stood up to leave.

And besides, I told Teresa I was coming. I wouldn't want to disappoint her. After all, I am a man of my word.

I found my way back to my room, washed up, slapped on some cologne, and then headed for the parking structure to retrieve my rental car. I fumbled for my keys as I went to unlock the door. It seemed more difficult than normal. 'Why do they keep this garage so dimly lit?' I thought. Once inside, I started the car and put its convertible top down. It was a warm summer night, perfect for cruising. I started down the circular ramp and by the time I reached the street level I was thoroughly dizzy. I closed my eyes for a sec before entering traffic. When I opened them again everything had stopped orbiting. I made the right turn into what seemed like a stampede of cows heading off to slaughter. Somebody honked. Then somebody else honked. 'Where'd all these rude, impatient people come from,' I thought.

"Where'd you get your license?" one hothead yelled out to me. "A toy store?"

"California, buddy," I yelled back as I accelerated past him. I looked down at my watch. It was only seven something. 'Doing good,' I thought. 'Don't want to keep Teresa waiting.' I looked back up and…

"Oh my…" WHAM!!

Everything went black.

Meanwhile, back at her hotel, Teresa waited. She had a chilled bottle of bubbly delivered to her room. She'd also slipped into something more comfortable. Soft music played on her radio. The lights were dimmed. The electric fireplace was turned on low for ambiance. Teresa sat expectantly on the sofa, ready to celebrate the night away.

An hour and fifteen minutes went by teasingly slow.

'Mark sure isn't in a hurry,' Teresa thought.

An hour and a half went by.

'Knowing the kind of guy Mark is, he probably stopped to buy me flowers or a box of chocolates. He's so thoughtful,' she reasoned, not wanting to think that I might not show.

Two hours went by.

Teresa got up and began pacing the room.

"I can't believe it. Where is he? This is not like Mark. He's always so prompt. Oh, I feel like such a fool!" Teresa chastised herself out-loud. "I CAN'T BELIEVE I BARED MY SOUL TO HIM, MADE MYSELF VULNERABLE. AND NOW, NOW HE'S CHANGED HIS MIND. HE'S STOOD ME UP! HE'S REJECTED ME! AAGH!!"

There was a knock at the door. "Hotel security. Is everything all right in there?"

"NO I'M NOT ALL RIGHT. I JUST MADE AN ASS OUT OF MYSELF! MAN, AM I STUPID!" she hollered through the door. "I'M SORRY, I'LL KEEP IT QUIET NOW. AAGH!" Teresa plopped down onto the sofa, picked up the phone on the end table, and dialed for room service, "Would you please send a large box of assorted chocolates up to my room." 'To heck with my figure tonight, I deserve this,' she rationalized. Seems like a whole lotta rationalizing was going on this night.

Later, while watching TV with empty chocolate wrappers scattered all around her, the eleven o'clock news came on. The first story involved a horrific crash with fatalities earlier that evening. Two survivors, both in critical condition, had been rushed to the hospital. There was still no further word on their condition or as to the cause of the accident. "Oh, no!" Teresa screamed in shock. There, behind the reporter, was what looked to be my rental car. She quickly got dressed and rushed out the door.

"I refuse to help that guy. He repulses me. He makes me sick!" I heard someone say in the background. I couldn't see anything but I could hear voices.

"Betty, you're a nurse first when in here. You're a professional. You need to check your feelings at the door. Now get over there and tend to that patient."

"I'm sorry doctor, I can't."

"What do you mean, you can't," an elevated perturbed voice replied.

"Five years ago a drunk driver killed my twin sister. I cannot guarantee this guy will get my best treatment. For all I care he can die and rot in hell."

"Okay, switch positions with Marge. We'll talk about this later."

A few minutes after, Marge entered the room. There were tears in her eyes. "Dr. Johnson, the girl just passed. We couldn't save her," she informed in a hushed tone.

"Damn! Sometimes I hate this job. When are people going to learn, drinking and driving don't mix, they kill."

I opened my eyes. 'What am I doing here?' I thought. What was that talk all about? Why am I wearing an oxygen mask?' I was confused.

Teresa saw me open my eyes and hurried to my bedside. "Thank God! You're alive!" she exclaimed. "You're going to be all right."

"What happened?" I asked.

"You were in an accident. I saw it on the news and came right here to the hospital to be with you. I've been here all night."

"What time is it?"

"It's noon," she answered. Then, bending over, Teresa kissed me on the forehead and whispered in my ear, "By the way, I told them I was your wife. It was the only way they'd let me stay. I was so worried about you. I couldn't leave you here alone."

Dr. Johnson and nurse Marge saw that I had regained consciousness and came over to check on me. They took my blood pressure, checked my other vital signs, and then removed the oxygen mask.

"How are you feeling?" the doctor asked.

"My head hurts," I replied.

"That it should. You've suffered a concussion. We're giving you something for the pain. Do you remember what happened?" he questioned.

"The last thing I remember is turning right out of a parking structure and then waking up here just a few moments ago. Who ran into me?"

Not wanting to answer, he skirted the question. "Let's simply say that you were more fortunate than the others, especially since you weren't wearing a seatbelt. You were thrown from your car and landed on your head. You could have been paralyzed, or worse, killed."

"That didn't answer my question. Who ran into me and what..."?

The ICU door flung open.

"Mark, where are you? We have to talk." It was Chelsea.

Marge intercepted her before she reached my bed. "I'm sorry, ma'am, but you'll have to wait outside. We have a one visitor at a time rule here in ICU and Mr. Manion's wife is visiting with him right now."

"Excuse me! I'm Mrs. Manion, Mr. Manion's wife. Who's this floozy?" my wife demanded angrily.

Tension mounted in the room. The air got heavy. Maybe I needed to be back on oxygen. And then a humorous thought struck me a la the show What's My Line, 'Will the real Mrs. Manion please stand up.' I know, how could I think of something like that at a time like this? The answer, a warped mind in an awkward situation.

Teresa excused herself, "I'm sorry. I'm not really his wife, just a concerned business associate of his. I didn't want Mark to be left alone and they wouldn't let me in otherwise. I'll leave now."

Chelsea got right in my face, "Can't be left alone, eh? How 'bout me? You left me alone at home with those two monsters. Who is she, Mark? The truth, who is she really?"

"A business associate. She's just a concerned business associate," I replied. "Now let's start over, okay? Hi, dear. How are you? Where are the boys?"

"Where are the boys? Is that all you care about? I came all this way to see you and all you can ask is where are the boys?"

"No, dear, first I ..."

"Are you arguing with me already?"

"No, dear, I..."

"Now you're arguing with me about arguing with me. You're never going to change, are you? Well, are you?"

I closed my eyes. 'This can't really be happening,' I thought. I kept hearing are you?, are you?, are you?, like a broken record. I opened my eyes again. She was really here raking me over the coals.

"How much did you have to drink on the flight here?" I asked. "You know it messes with your medications."

"Who made you the alcohol cop? You have no right to get on my case, you who just killed three people."

"No way."

"Yes way. Why do you think there's a policeman standing right outside your door? Ain't no passing go, you are going straight to jail."

"That can't be true."

"Think again. I talked to the policeman. He told me that you killed a mother, a father, and a child. That makes you a murderer, a mass murderer."

'So that's what I overheard earlier,' I thought. 'No way. This can't be happening. I'm not that kind of guy. There's a good chance my wife is mistaken. After all, look at her, she's wasted.' I was in extreme denial.

"I'll have you know, you've murdered my life now too," my wife went on. "What am I going to do with two boys? You know I wanted girls. Why didn't you give me girls? Who's going to take care of me?"

"Somehow it'll all work out," I said without believing a word of it.

"It better or I'm filing for divorce. I can't live alone. I'll find somebody else. You better get a good attorney to get you off or it's over, we're done."

It's strange, but that part of it had some appeal. All the years of verbal abuse and being used as her punching bag would be over. That could be a bright spot. I knew the majority of the abuse was misplaced anger, but it hurt nonetheless. It was hard to live with. More importantly, right now though, was the awareness that was beginning to sink in, the awareness that I may have killed three people. I heard the hospital staff talking; I saw the policeman looking in at me; I understood what my wife had said, even though she was looped. I could put two and two together. I wasn't a total idiot. I could even remember what the instructor said at a class I had to attend after my last DUI arrest. He said that if we didn't change our behavior there's a good chance we'd wind up killing somebody. 'Yeah, right,' I thought, 'that would never happen to me.' Now three innocent lives had been cut short, and probably by me. I blew it, big time! I could already feel the weight of that pulling me down. It felt like my heart was being shredded. The guilt …the shame …how was I going to be able to live with myself now?

A few hours later I was released into the custody of the policeman. He read me my rights, "You have the right to remain silent. …" etc., handcuffed me, loaded me into the back of his policecar, and then hauled me off to jail. At the jail I was booked in under the suspicion of felony drunk driving. Suspicion … hmm?

Chapter Twelve

Another of Life's Trials

The following month went by excruciatingly slow. I'd been bailed out of jail on a $25,000 bond which was paid for by my company, ODD. I was surprised that they'd want to help me after some of the negative publicity they received. I had really tarnished their name. Tabloid headlines like, 'Sub Guy Torpedoes Family' and 'ODDD, Our Deli Delivers Death' blared from newsstands. Then there were the sick jokes that found their way to talk show television. They were merciless. 'What do you call a drunk driver who kills, not two, but three people? ODD.' Strangely enough, they still didn't want to lose my services. Teresa remained my staunch ally. She persuaded them to pay for a high-powered attorney to represent me. 'Why?' I thought. I was guilty. I was loaded, a .16 BAC (blood alcohol content) level, way over the legal limit for driving. I killed three people. Where was the suspicion in that? It happened. Fact. I felt horrible. I probably did deserve to rot in hell.

The attorney thought he'd found a loophole, a way out no matter what. It had something to do with the way they'd drawn my blood and tested it for alcohol content. He only wanted to use it if it looked like his first plan of defense wasn't working. I met with him at his office. There he explained his strategy. His name was Perry.

"I want you to answer any questions about the crash with, 'I don't remember' or 'I don't know,'" Perry instructed. "The concussion you received will validate that response."

"But what if I do remember?" I questioned. "My memory of the crash came back. In fact, I've been having nightmares reliving it. In my nightmares I look up, see a blurry red light, and bam, I hit something."

"Nightmares are simply dreams. And dreams are imaginations. And imaginations are stories or ideas our brains conjure up. You can't be sure they're true. You don't want to end up in prison on a mis-truth do you?"

"Well, no, but…"

"No buts. It was an accident, wasn't it?" he continued.

"Well, yes, but…"

"You shouldn't have to do prison time for an accident. Besides, you don't remember. The sun was going down at that time of day. It might have blinded you where you couldn't see the stoplight."

"That could have played a part," I agreed.

"I don't think you saw the light because of the sun. I'm telling you, I'm good. I know what I'm doing. Just follow my instructions," Perry said confidently. "I can get you off. At worst, you may get a year of probation and possibly have to do fifty hours of community service."

The idea of not going to prison was appealing. Being incarcerated would surely put a damper on my life. My career would take a hit. My boys would surely get worse with mom raising them alone. They may even be fully grown and have moved out by the time I get released. And then, yowser, I wouldn't get to ski or play tennis. It'd be so confining. I learned my lesson. What good would incarceration do me or anybody else?

Being the expert rationalizer that I was, I began telling myself why I didn't deserve prison. I started buying into what my attorney had said. I went on a shopping spree of thoughts to justify my defense, my freedom. But it was as if I was using counterfeit money. As hard as I mentally tried to clear my conscience I still had a guilty feeling gnawing deep inside. The trial was only a few days away. What was the right thing to do? What would I do?

The day of the trial arrived. Before entering the courtroom my attorney had one more thing to say.

"Trust me," he said. "I will get you off. Just answer the questions the way I instructed you to."

The courtroom was packed. The family that I'd permanently laid to rest had been very active and well-respected in this community. The father was a fireman. He was on the town council and coached his daughter's softball team. The mother was a stay-at-home mom, a Sunday-school teacher and Girl Scout leader. She worked in the snack bar at her daughter's games. Their daughter was a cute ten-year-old blonde girl with pigtails. She was a gold star student, played softball and soccer, and took piano lessons. Recently she'd had a lemonade stand to raise money for Special Olympics. She was a parents' dream child. I already knew all this from how the family was portrayed in newspaper articles after the crash. Oops! There I go using the word crash. Perry told me not to use that word, not to even think that word, that it sounded too harsh. Always, always use the word accident when referring to my unfortunate mishap, he'd advised. It's softer. 'Mind games', I thought.

Opening arguments were made by both sides. The prosecuting attorney painted a lousy portrait of me. He told the jury that I was an alcoholic with two prior DUIs. He told them about my dysfunctional family as a result of my drinking, how I'd negatively contributed to my wife's struggle with drugs and alcohol, about my two very young boys who'd already been in trouble for underage drinking. "The apple doesn't fall far from the tree," he said. "Mr. Manion has not been a good example to his wife or his children. He is the head of a family spinning out of control. And now, masking his problems behind excessive drinking, and driving under that influence, his irresponsible action has killed three innocent victims. One, a child, just ten years old, at the beginning of her life. Mr. Manion is guilty of felony drunk driving."

My defense attorney must've gone to a different art school than the prosecutor because he painted an entirely different picture of me. His contrasting opinion left me feeling like a Jekyll and Hyde candidate. He told the jury what an outstanding husband and father I was. He told them about my hard work ethic. How I used that money to support my family, to pay for my wife's expensive rehab programs, for guitar and tennis lessons for my boys, and to keep a nice roof over their heads. My attorney was good. By the time he was done talking about me he practically had me walking on water. He told them how sorry I was, but that it was an accident, an accident that could've happened to any one of them. "I'm sure you can all remember sometime in your driving experience," he told them, "when you were temporarily blinded by the sunlight coming through your windshield. In a way, Mark here is also a victim, a victim of that blinding light. The accident was just that, an accident. My client is innocent."

I was the first person called to the witness stand by the prosecuting attorney. I looked out at all the people who'd come. They loved that family I'd killed. They were there because they wanted to see justice served. I saw my wife eyeing me intently from the back of the courtroom. I could hear her thoughts by the way she looked at me. 'You better win, stay out of prison or else,' is what her eyes said. Perry, my attorney, sat there smugly at his table, confident that he'd win my case.

Then I looked over at the picture of the ten-year-old girl. Dang, she was cute. I thought back to when I was in fourth grade. She would have been the kind of girl I'd have had a crush on. I remembered what that age was like. My favorite teacher growing up had been my fourth-grade teacher, Mr. Jones. I remembered building a paper-mache volcano in his class, one that actually erupted. I remembered when Mr. Jones asked Sue, the girl sitting next to me, to use the word "tinkle" in a sentence. "Mr. Jones tinkled on the floor," she responded with a grin. The class roared with laughter. Mr. Jones did too. The girl in the picture looked a lot like Sue. I remembered playing hopscotch and dodge-ball. I remembered playing the clarinet in the school orchestra. There's been so much life lived since then. And that cute little girl in the picture would never get to experience it.

"Will you please state your full name for the record?" the prosecuting attorney asked.

"My name is Mark Manion. Mark is with a k. Then Manion, M A N I O N, sounds like canyon but with an m."

"Will you please tell the court what happened just prior to the crash?" was his next question.

"You mean accident, don't you?" I queried back. "I never meant to kill anyone. It was an accident." Perry nodded.

"Just answer the question," the Judge directed.

"Okay, Your Honor." I knew what my answer was supposed to be: 'I don't remember.' I looked at Perry. He nodded his head again with one of those go-ahead-and-say-it looks. I looked back over at the picture of the little girl. My mind went into rapid-fire rationalization. Sure I was guilty, but I'd suffered a lot already. There was the huge hit on my reputation, the bad PR to my company, and the heavy guilt feelings I had and would always have to deal with for the rest of my life. And my boys needed me. And what good is there in sending me to prison? It won't bring that family back.

"Mr. Manion, will you please answer the question?" the judge repeated.

I took one last look at the picture. Those pigtails. That smile. Her... A tsunami of grief over what I had done flooded my mind.

"I'm guilty, Your Honor."

A scream burst out from the back of the courtroom. It was my wife. In shock, she fainted and slumped down in her chair. Then there was a moment of stunned silence before my attorney jumped to his feet. He, too, seemed shocked.

"Your Honor, I move that that be stricken from the record," he said.

"On what grounds?"

"My client does not understand what he is saying. He suffered a concussion in the accident. It's affecting his ability to think straight, to comprehend."

"Is this true?" the judge asked me.

"I did get a concussion, Your Honor, but I'm over it. I know full well what I'm doing."

"But, Your Honor, my ..." Perry pushed.

"Sit down Counsel!" the judge ordered. "Motion denied. We will hear what Mr. Manion has to say." He motioned me to continue.

"It's clear and simple," I went on. "I was loaded. I had too much to drink and shouldn't have been driving. I looked down at my watch to see what time it was and when I looked back up all I saw was a red blur and, wham, there was the crash. Three fine people are now dead because of me. I am sorry. It was my fault. I won't ask for leniency or forgiveness because I don't deserve it. I will accept whatever punishment the court dishes out. Again, I am so, so very sorry."

My attorney, Perry, with elbows on his desk and hands holding his head, grimaced in disbelief. This hadn't gone the way he'd planned. He leered at me in disgust. 'You traitor, look what you've done to me,' I could hear him thinking.

I bowed my head. What had I just done?

The following day I was sentenced to nine years in state prison. An odd number for the ODD guy.

The steel barred door clanged shut behind me. I could hear the click as the warden turned the key in the latch. I was locked in. This was it, my new home. It didn't take long to get acquainted with my surroundings. They were sparse. The cell was a puny six feet by nine feet. It only contained a bunkbed, a stainless steel toilet with a sink directly above it and a polished metal mirror on the wall above that. On one side wall was a small desk and chair. On the other stood a less-than-spacious metal cabinet to store the few clothes I was issued. I was moving into a cell with another prisoner. I prayed he was nice.

A head with a big honker of a nose glanced over at me from the top bunk. You'd a thought it'd be bandaged. I mean, living in such tight quarters, how could one avoid scraping it on a wall or banging it into something? I was tempted to ask him what he was in for but I didn't want to appear nosy.

"You must be my new cellmate," he said.

"I guess so. My name's Mark," I responded.

"That'll be easy to remember. It's the second book of the New Testament, you know, in the Bible. Matthew, Mark."

My roommate jumped down from his bunk. He was buff! Not in the buff, Garden of Eden style, but buff in the sense that clearly he'd been pumping a lot of iron in a gym. He didn't look like he was one to be messed with.

"What do you call a guy who's missing both legs and an arm, and you throw him in a swimming pool?" he went on.

"I don't know," I answered. "What do you call him?"

"Bob!" he exclaimed while moving his arm up and down. "That's my name. Bob, only around here they call me Rev. Welcome." He reached out his hand and greeted me with a smile.

I breathed a sigh of relief.

Bob and I seemed to hit it off. He was a personable guy, very likeable. When he told me he was a Christian, that he became one years earlier, soon after entering prison, it made me feel more at ease. Why? Because I too claimed to be one. I was. 'If I'm a Christian, though, how'd I end up here?' I thought. I began to explain myself away to Bob but was cut short.

"You don't need to justify yourself to me. I get it. We're all sinners. Everybody in the world is. And if somebody says they aren't, they make God out to be a liar because it tells us in Romans 3:23, 'for all have sinned and fall short of the glory of God.' All of us. That's the reason God sent Jesus into this world. John 3:16 says, 'For God so loved the world that He gave His one and only Son, that whoever believes in Him should not perish but have everlasting life.' You see, when Jesus was crucified, when He died on that cross, He carried all our sin on His shoulders. He took our place. He who knew no sin became our sin. The Bible talks about that in 2 Corinthians 5:21. He was the perfect sacrifice. You gotta believe, though, It tells us, 'Believe in the Lord Jesus Christ and you will be saved.' That's Acts 16:31."

"Preach it, Rev," I heard from a nearby cell. "You got the fire!"

Bob had a captive audience.

"You gotta have faith," he continued. "Romans 10:17 says, 'Consequently, faith comes from hearing the message, and the message is heard through the word of Christ.' And God's word will not return void. That's Isaiah 55:11 in a nutshell. And grab a hold of this one. Joel 2:32 says, 'And everyone who calls on the name of the Lord will be saved,' That's for me and for you brother."

I listened intently because a small voice inside me told me I needed to. I hadn't even sat down yet and I was being sermonized. Would it leave a sheen? Bob sure was excited about what he was saying. He spoke with confidence, conviction, like he meant every word of it.

"I'm going before a parole board in a few months and have a good chance of getting out early. I've learned my lesson the hard way. You'd think that would be enough but I know better. Prison doors are like revolving doors. Many who get out wind up right back in. It's easy to resume the old ways once you get out. In Matthew, chapter 7, verses

13 and 14 we are warned, 'Enter through the narrow gate, for wide is the gate and broad is the road that leads to destruction, and many enter through it. But small is the gate and narrow the road that leads to life, and only a few find it.'"

"Amen," another prisoner shouted out. "Tell it like it is." Several others clapped their hands in approval. The prison walls had ears.

"We'll all be tempted to do things that aren't right, that go against God's ways. It'll happen when we get out. It even happens here in the box. But God is good! He assures us in his word in 1 Corinthians 10:13 that, 'No temptation has seized you except what is common to man. And God is faithful; he will not allow you to be tempted beyond what you can bear. But when you are tempted, he will also provide a way out so that you can stand up under it.' We'll still have to choose, the right way or the wrong way. Myself, I know I'll have to be careful because I know I'm no different than anybody else. I'm not infallible. I'll need to make the right choices too, obey what I've learned, or risk coming back here. Worse yet is being out of sorts with God. Sin has consequences."

"No fooling," I finally interjected. "And me, I should've known better. I made a commitment to follow Christ at an early age. I read my Bible. I knew right from wrong. But noooo, I started wanting to do things my way, not God's way. I got off track, and here I am. My life's in shambles."

"How'd that happen?" Bob asked.

Bob probably wished he hadn't asked that question because it began a three-hour discourse on my life. I felt safe talking to him. He listened patiently while I rambled on. Occasionally Bob would jot down something on a piece of paper. It turned out to be Bible references he thought might help me. I was impressed by that.

"Man, you are one smart fellow," I commented.

"Then why am I in here?"

"I mean I can't get over how much you know the Bible."

"I've had years to study it, to reflect on it, to see where I've fallen short in my own life."

"By the way, if you don't mind my asking, why are you in here?"

"I strangled somebody who got too nosy," he said with a deadpan expression. "I don't know what happened. I just snapped. My psychiatrist thinks I might be better now."

There was an awkward pause. He seemed so real. Then he grinned. "Just teasin'. Why I'm here, that's a whole 'nother story. Someday I'll share it with you."

"Lights out!!" yelled the prison guard as he walked the corridor. "It's bedtime. Keep it down in here."

Bob hopped back onto the top bunk. I got the one below. This brought a question to my mind as I laid there staring up at the mattress above. "Yo, Rev, you're not a bed-wetter are you?"

"I guess you'll know in the morning," he responded. "Makes me think of another verse for you. In 1 Thessalonians 5:16,17, and 18 it says to 'Be joyful always, pray continually, give thanks in all circumstances, for this is God's will for you in Christ Jesus.'"

What was I going to find out in the morning? I closed my eyes and fell asleep while praying, thanking God for my cellmate. Yes, what would tomorrow have in store?

Chapter Thirteen

A Siren Sounds

The piercing sound of a siren could be heard in the background. I didn't want to open my eyes. Thoughts of prison riots, stabbings, and all sorts of mayhem went through my mind. I'd heard about police in riot gear storming prisons, batons drawn and tear gas being set off. Of fires. Of innocent hostages being killed. Wrong place, wrong time. Please, not on my first day I prayed. Then I opened my eyes. It was bright. The lights were on. Two paramedics from the fire department had just arrived and were crouching by my side. It was surreal, but I knew right away where I was. I was at Little Caesars© where I was supposed to be picking up my pizzas.

"You're going to be okay, we're here," one of the paramedics said reassuringly. "Did you lose consciousness?"

"I don't think so. I simply closed my eyes for a minute hoping that this would all go away. That it would just be a bad dream."

"You're not dreaming. Your head took a hard blow. Now try to remain still. We're going to put this brace around your neck to keep it stable. We're also going to slide this board underneath you and strap you to it to keep your spine aligned. I hope these aren't your best slacks."

"Why's that?" I asked.

"The duck-tape we are using will likely fray or put a hole in them," he answered.

"Just go for it."

Another siren could be heard approaching. It was the ambulance to transport me to the hospital. A crowd of onlookers watched curiously. I didn't think to charge any of them a fee for their front row seats to the reality show that was my life. I had other things on my mind.

What If Resolved

Why did I write this book? I wrote it because many times over the last 46 years of my physically challenged existence people have felt sorry for me. They've seen my struggles and felt I didn't get a fair shake at life. If only this or if only that, I'd hear. Life could be and would have been so much better for you, so much easier. But would it have been?

At age 19 I seemed to have the world by the tail. I excelled at both school and athletics, was in great physical shape, and was a hard worker. I had lofty aspirations of climbing the corporate ladder. I loved to compete. I was both a thinker and a doer. My future looked very promising. Then, on August 7, 1974, at about ten o'clock at night, life as I knew it ceased to exist.

Mike and I indeed were struck by a drunk driver that night outside of Bakersfield. It wasn't a dream. Mike really was killed and I really was left totally paralyzed from the neck down. You can read about it in my first book, "Unfinished Miles, One Man's Unthinkable Journey." That night I went from a fiercely independent individual who thought he could do almost anything to one who was completely dependent on others for everything, even breathing. I spent the next ten months in the hospital. It took several years and lots of effort, but with the help of outstanding doctors, superb therapists, and bucket loads of prayer, I actually recovered to the point where I could walk with a cane. Miracles really do happen. Like Mike, I too should have been dead.

And then on January 13, 1991, I really did break my neck again at Little Caesars©. I lost more feeling and function, and could no longer use a cane to get around. The use of a wheelchair or a walker became necessary. Even so, my rehab doctor was still amazed at how well I was doing considering all I'd been through. He counted it a near miracle. I managed to stay mostly independent except for my driving. That I chose to give up in 1995 after a couple of harrowing experiences. It was a hard thing to do. It felt like quitting and I hated that, but I didn't want to be responsible for hurting or killing anyone else.

In the Spring of 2001 I needed another major surgery. Fluid was amassing at the top of my spine, and a bit lower a bone spur appeared to be compressing my spinal cord. I was losing more physical ability. It was going to be a difficult operation, my neurologist informed. He warned me that I could end up on a respirator for the rest of my life and lose my ability to speak. Many prayed, and thank God, mums not the word, my voice was left intact. However, I did lose more motor function and my independence. Since then I've required a caregiver.

I commemorated the Fall of 2010 with another fall. It was a freak accident. At night, in the dark, I rolled off a curb in my wheelchair and landed head first in the street. It wasn't pretty. I gashed my head, cracked my shoulder, injured two more vertebrae, and strained the muscles in my neck. I felt like such an idiot. How could I have allowed this to happen to me? I hadn't been drinking and I wasn't on any drugs. Once again, as I often have done, I looked at the verse I have mounted above my desk. I may not always feel it, but God does say, "Blessed is the man who perseveres under trial, because when he has stood the test, he will receive the crown of life that God has promised to those that love him." (James 1:12) I'm banking on it. Shortly after that incident I got a power wheelchair.

Oh crap! In writing this it reminds me of a bet I made with one of my best friends, Greg. He's also a quadriplegic. Way back when we used to compete in wheelchair athletics, track and field, the bet was made. We both used manual wheelchairs then. The bet was on which one of us would resort to using an electric wheelchair first. I lost. It's sad, but when I told Greg he'd won he couldn't remember what the bet was for, and neither could I. I hope that doesn't make me a welcher. Older age is creeping in.

Breaking my neck twice, undergoing a dozen surgeries, my daily struggles with tasks that most people take for granted, losing my independence, and now this bet, are all consequences of that fateful August night. That crash still affects me and will for the rest of my life. It keeps on giving. Come to think of it, tediously typing the entirety of this book and two others having to use only one finger is another consequence. So, I ask myself the question like others have — what if? What if the crash hadn't happened? What if I could have a do over? Would I take it?

(long pause)

Hey, I'm thinking.

It's tempting. I'll tell you, I miss downhill skiing and tennis and racquetball. I miss bicycling and running and swimming and backpacking. Shooting hoops, catching passes, and kicking goals are now found only in my dreams. Sounds crazy, but I miss being able to mow a lawn or paint a house. I miss being able to jump out of bed in the morning and get myself dressed. I miss eating a hamburger without total concentration. With my loss of feeling it's hard to tell how tightly I'm holding one. Squeeze too much and it squishes all over the place, not enough and it ends up in my lap or on the floor. Getting change out of a pocket is a cruel joke. Going to the bathroom, I need assistance. It's humbling. The list goes on and on. I've barely scratched the surface. And so, I contemplate a little longer. What if? Would I?

(short pause)

The answer is a resounding no. Who am I to question what God has allowed in my life? Had I not gotten injured, who knows, maybe my life would have turned out like the story in this book. There were times in my youth when I drove under the influence or was a passenger in a car with a driver who was. That's just plain stupid. I darn well could've killed or hurt someone myself, much like the guys that crashed into me and my cousin. "There but by the grace of God go I." In my defense I could say organizations like MADD and SADD didn't exist back then. The dangers of drinking and driving weren't hammered into us at school or on newscasts like they are today. Back then who ever heard of such a thing as a designated driver? Still, I knew better. It was a selfish choice, one that didn't take into consideration how it might effect others. Shame on me.

Next, if I hadn't gotten wrecked up I probably would not be doing the public speaking that I do. Over the last 28 years I've had the opportunity to share my story with hundreds of thousands of people. It's a message of encouragement, of hope, of overcoming the challenges we will all face in life. It's also one about choices and their consequences, especially in regards to drinking, driving, and drugs. Speaking from my wheelchair makes a strong visual statement. I speak at military bases, schools, rehab centers, churches, and ... well, if a door opens, I try and make it work.

Why do I do it? It's certainly not for the money, almost all of my talks are done at no charge. I do it because I love people and care about what happens to them. I do it because I truly believe it's one of the reasons God spared my life. That does not make me a saint. Believe me, there have been times when I felt like — how can I put it nicely — like a cow paddy. My body will be at war with itself. I'll be achy, can barely keep my head up, and my emotions have been trounced upon. It's been a bad day physically and mentally. On the way to that talk I question what I'm doing. Am I just wasting my time? Does anybody really care? Does it make a difference? I balk at going yet I muster up the energy and give my presentation anyway. And almost always, without fail, someone or a bunch of someones will approach me afterwards and tell me how much the talk impacted them. Some needed a boost in their spirit. Others had been on a path that leads to destruction and promised to mend their ways. I leave with tears in my eyes, apologizing to God for my bad attitude. I'm reminded that attitude usually determines one's altitude in life, so I try to pick a good one.

Years ago I got an e-mail from someone who heard me speak and read my first book. She said I must be proud that God had enough faith in me to entrust me with such a powerful story. I cried. It gave me a new perspective on what's happened to me. I've embraced that thought ever since. I've been entrusted. I have a responsibility. On the surface my situation can seem awful, but good has come from it. People have been inspired. Lives have been changed, better choices made. If I can make it, they can make it. Good has come from my tragedy. "And we know that in all things God works for the good of those who love him, who have been called according to his purpose." (Romans 8:28)

Lastly, here is my favorite reason for not wanting a do over. If I hadn't been hurt in that crash I never would have met my wife. Although now divorced, I would have missed the good times we did have and the beautiful music that filled our home. Our two precious daughters would not exist. Banish the thought!! I also would not have met many other wonderful people over the years. My life has been so enriched by them. I would never go back and risk our paths not crossing. Those friendships are cherished possessions. My family, my neighbors, and all my other friends are like a masterpiece of art that God has blessed me with. It has a prominent place in my heart. Some have told me not to hesitate in calling if I need anything, that they'd be there for me. And they have. Whoa, that gives me an idea for another song. 'You just call out my name, and you know wherever I am, I'll come running ... .' Just kidding once again. Been done. Carole King penned those lyrics on her 'You've Got a Friend' hit in 1971. You didn't think I'd end this book without some more of my nonsense, did you? Thanks for reading it.

Peace be with you, *Mark*

And please, do not drink and drive.

CPSIA information can be obtained
at www.ICGtesting.com
Printed in the USA
FSHW022318090221

9 781593 309861